THE BEST IN

# POINT-OF-PURCHASE

# DESIGN

This book is for return on or before the last date shown below

THE BEST IN

# POINT-OF-PURCHASE

# DESIGN

STAFFORD CLIFF

ROTOVISION

A QUARTO BOOK

Published by ROTOVISION SA
Route Suisse 9
CH-1295 Mies
Switzerland

Distributed to the trade in the
United States by
Watson-Guptill Publications
1515 Broadway
New York, NY 10036

ISBN 0-8230-6169-8

This book was designed and produced by
Quarto Publishing plc
6 Blundell Street
London N7 9BH

Creative Director: Richard Dewing
Designer: Chris Dymond
Editor: Susan Berry
Picture Researcher: Michele Faram

Typeset in Great Britain by
Central Southern Typesetters, Eastbourne
Manufactured in Hong Kong by Regent Publishing Services Limited
Printed in Hong Kong by Leefung-Asco Printers Ltd

Stafford Cliff would like to acknowledge the help of the following
people in the compilation of this book: Jeremy Schwartz, Fran Bell,
Juliette Gouriat, Barry David Berger, Jonathan Scott, Stephen Paul, Alan
McDougal, James Pyott, Bernard Dooling, Brian Wright and Bruce
Heyhoe.

# Contents

**Introduction**        6

**Window Display Material**        10

**Floor-Standing Units**        60

**Counter-top Promotions**        86

**Product Dispensers**        142

**Co-ordinated Schemes**        176

**In-store Systems**        190

Index of Projects        222

Directory of Practising Designers        223

# Introduction

Every brand manager and marketing manager knows the meaning of point of purchase. A friend of mine, who works as a brand manager for a major chocolate manufacturer, defines it as promoting a product, "making the maximum use of the minimum amount of space, preferably using space in store that was not otherwise occupied, and preferably (in his case) as close to the till as possible."

Point of purchase can be a much more cost-effective way of increasing product sales and, more importantly in times of recession, a much more definable and recordable way to spend the promotion budget than advertising or posters. And it is an area that is constantly changing, as new materials are developed and new products emerge.

Products such as video sales, which did not exist 10 years ago, are now one of the prime users of point-of-purchase material internationally. With all this opportunity, why is it that point of purchase still has such a bad image among designers? And why is it so hard to find good creative examples of the medium?

**Poor relation**  A few years ago, if you asked a design company to undertake a point-of-purchase project, you might be confronted by embarrassment and shuffling of feet, or, at the very least, you might detect slight nose-wrinkling as they ask if they can also tackle the brand identity or the packaging.

Compared with other areas of design, point of purchase has always been the poor relation, often left to printers or packaging specialists, or the brand managers themselves. But with most of the Western world in the grip of a recession, design companies cannot afford to be so choosy. Clients spend less money on advertising — looking instead for a more immediate return on their investment. At the same time, retailers are looking at additional ways to move merchandise.

**What is point of purchase?**  A design team, working on a new retail concept, or the redesign of an existing store, will consider point of purchase to mean all of the in-store graphics. High-level product identification, descriptive and directional signs, promotion and price ticketing, labelling on products, and shelf-edge signs might all be considered as some form of point of purchase. And along with this comes the flexibility to move products around, change the look of the store seasonally, introduce sale and Christmas graphics, and marry the whole package to the exterior identity of the shop or, in some cases, the retail chain.

Point of purchase, unless very carefully considered at the outset, can easily undermine (or even destroy) the image and unity of the store or the integrity of the product.

So we have two types of point of purchase; one produced by the retailer and one by the manufacturer. A retailer who has spent a great deal of time and money creating and maintaining the look of his store will often now allow manufacturers or suppliers to use their own point of purchase. But there is also a third type of point of purchase, one which serves not only to promote the product, but to package and protect it as well. As costs of packaging increase and manufacturers and customers become more environmentally aware, they are looking at ways of combining the outer protective carrier of the product, with the inner display container or dispenser. In future, products sent to small independent retailers (where most traditional point-of-purchase occurs) might arrive in packs that can be adapted, cut open or folded back to go straight into the shop.

**The way forward** This is a fresh challenge that will not be met by the graphic designer alone. It will take the skills of the manufacturer, the industrial designer and the package specialist to come up with new and truly innovative solutions.

As more and more manufacturers merge and combine, it is easy to imagine a time when a store will consist of only the basic shell – walls, lighting and, perhaps, signage. Shelving might comprise very basic fixtures, into which the manufacturers' own merchandizing modules would fit, adapted and tailor-made for each product.

This book is not a comprehensive survey of every type of point of purchase that exists, or has ever been produced. It is a selection of the most interesting solutions to the widest possible cross-section of briefs, which I hope will provide inspiration to anyone about to undertake a point-of-purchase project themselves.

**Window display material** Some of the most creative display work over the last 20 years has been done by large department stores, who employ their own teams of designers to think up and then implement ideas to promote their product lines, draw people into their stores, and entertain passers-by. Who, as a child, has not been taken window shopping to see the Christmas displays? In New York, large stores even commission named artists to create fashion windows, and roped-off areas are set up on the sidewalk to allow people to file past these mechanically operated "magic kingdoms". Even limitations of size are not a restriction – Tiffany's tiny windows have long been famous for their creativity and imagination.

But stores with more than one outlet, chains of franchises all over the world, or manufacturers keen to provide material to attract attention to their product in otherwise unimaginative low-cost windows, must resort to mass-produced solutions: cardboard cut-outs, printed posters, and photographic blow-ups are the techniques most often utilized in this sector.

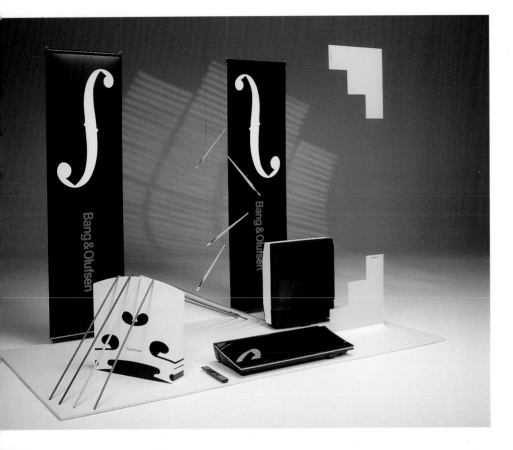

## The Art of Painting

**CLIENT:** Bang & Olufsen A/S, Struer, Denmark

**DESIGNER:** Studio John Boye, Struer, Denmark

**ILLUSTRATOR/PHOTOGRAPHER:** Ib Sorensen

**DATE OF COMPLETION:** Spring 1991

**TARGET MARKET:** Europe, USA, Canada, Asia

**PLACE OF SALE:** Bang & Olufsen's distribution and organization

**CLIENT'S BRIEF:** A generic window decoration for adaptation during the season 1991/2.

**DESIGN RATIONALE:** Art elements – like the forms from bowed string instruments – signal music. Another element, like colour, is also often used – here in the colours of the spectrum as strings over the violin chair. The paint brushes are suspended on thin threads to look like mobiles. Two backdrops with graphic symbols from a viola are used to attract attention.

## The Art of Music

**CLIENT:** Bang & Olufsen A/S, Struer, Denmark

**DESIGNER:** Studio John Boye, Struer, Denmark

**ILLUSTRATOR OR PHOTOGRAPHER:** Ib Sørensen, Struer, Denmark

**DATE OF COMPLETION:** Spring 1991

**TARGET MARKET:** Europe, USA, Canada and Asia

**PLACE OF SALE OF PRODUCT:** Bang & Olufsen's distribution and organization

**CLIENT'S BRIEF:** In connection with the jubilee year 1991 for Mozart's birthday, 'Modern Mozart' was chosen as the theme to emphasize that music is immortal. The window decoration follows a campaign with musical evenings all over the world with presentation of Mozart's music on Bang & Olufsen music systems.

**DESIGN RATIONALE:** Modern Mozart, but with old instruments. The theme was extended with the symphony as the visual concept. Instruments in pure graphic reproductions of black/white with the staircase element from the season. The window decoration is composed of several elements to make it adaptable for large and small windows.

## The Art of Ballet

**CLIENT:** Bang & Olufsen A/S, Struer, Denmark

**DESCRIPTION OF PRODUCT:** Window display

**DESIGNER:** Studio John Boye, Struer, Denmark

**ILLUSTRATOR OR PHOTOGRAPHER:** Ib Sørensen, Struer, Denmark

**DATE OF COMPLETION:** Spring 1991

**TARGET MARKET:** Europe, USA, Canada, Asia

**PLACE OF SALE:** Bang & Olufsen's distribution and organization

**CLIENT'S BRIEF:** A generic window decoration for the season 1991/92.

**DESIGN RATIONALE:** Music in other art forms – like here in ballet, represented by a pair of feet and legs, which are in a black/white print signal movement. The red bow at the bottom is another element from the ballet which together with the staircase signal "on the way up." The staircase is made of materials that can carry small products as shown on the illustration. Here terminals are shown for the operation of Bang & Olufsen products.

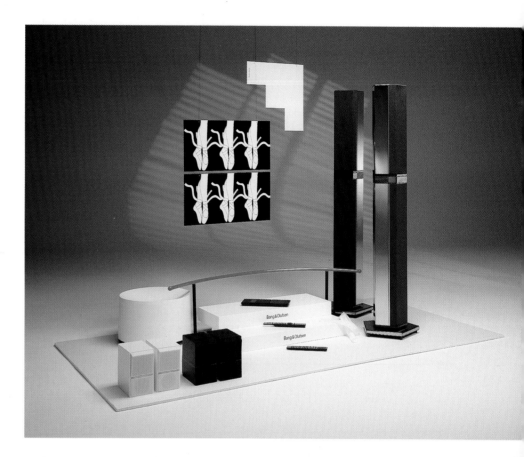

## The Art of Christmas

**CLIENT:** Bang & Olufsen, Struer, Denmark

**DESCRIPTION OF PRODUCT:** Window display

**DESIGNER:** Studio John Boye, Struer, Denmark

**ILLUSTRATOR OR PHOTOGRAPHER:** Ib Sørensen, Struer, Denmark

**DATE OF COMPLETION:** Spring 1991

**TARGET MARKET:** Europe, USA, Canada, Asia

**PLACE OF SALE:** Bang & Olufsen's distribution and organization

**CLIENT'S BRIEF:** Christmas window – with symbols that clearly signal Christmas 91/92.

**DESIGN RATIONALE:** To create purchase bags in beautiful materials, printed with Christmas symbols. The bags are suspended on a light metal stand forming a Christmas tree. The same Christmas elements are hung as mobiles from the ceiling.

## The Art of Writing

**CLIENT:** Bang & Olufsen A/S, Struer, Denmark

**DESIGNER:** Studio John Boye, Struer, Denmark

**DATE OF COMPLETION:** Spring 1991

**TARGET MARKET:** Europe, USA, Canada and Asia

**PLACE OF SALE OF PRODUCT:** Bang & Olufsen's distribution and organization

**CLIENTS' BRIEF:** A generic window decoration for adaptation to the whole 1992/93 season

**DESIGN RATIONALE:** The design language of Bang & Olufsen's window decoration often utilizes elements from the world of music, like the notes that signalize music and sound. The intention was to be able to extend the generic window from small to large windows.

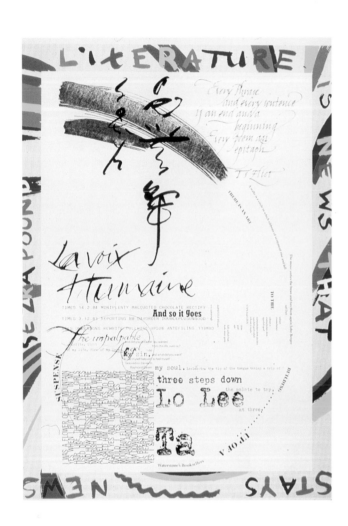

## Book Posters

**CLIENT:** Waterstones Booksellers, London, UK

**DESCRIPTION OF PRODUCT:** Posters on subject themes –
literature, travel, food, drink and gardening,
architecture, history and classical art, modern arts,
drama, philosophy and politics, Christmas

**DESIGNER:** Newell & Sorrell, London, UK

**DATE OF COMPLETION:** 1992

**TARGET MARKET:** Bookshop customers at Waterstone's
retail outlets

## Christmas Banners

**CLIENT:** Sherratt & Hughes, London, UK (now merged with Waterstones Ltd)

**DESCRIPTION OF PRODUCT:** Banners, catalogue, bookmarks and gift vouchers for bookshop

**DESIGNER:** Newell & Sorrell, London, UK

**ILLUSTRATOR:** Alan Cracknell

**DATE OF COMPLETION:** 1989

**TARGET MARKET:** Book shop customers

**CLIENT'S BRIEF:** To create a range of point-of-purchase material that would work on its own or as a set.

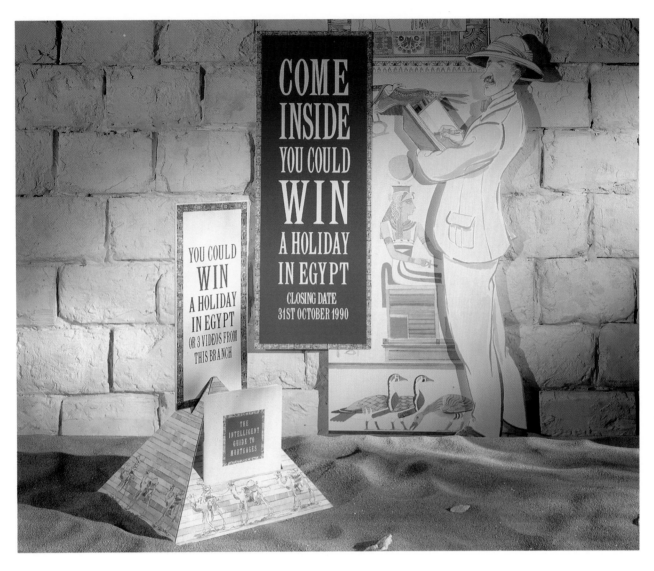

## 'Egypt' mortgage promotion

**CLIENT:** Bristol & West Building Society, Bristol, UK

**DESCRIPTION OF PRODUCT:** Window display and point-of-purchase units for branch network

**DESIGNER:** Proctor & Stevenson, Bristol, UK

**ILLUSTRATOR OR PHOTOGRAPHER:** Sue Shields

**DATE OF COMPLETION:** 1991

**TARGET MARKET:** All potential mortgage borrowers

**PLACE OF SALE:** Building Society branches

**CLIENT'S BRIEF:** Initially to design a booklet explaining the full range of mortgage services. This brief was subsequently developed by Proctor & Stevenson.

**DESIGN RATIONALE:** To ensure that the booklet was actually read and to attract potential new customers. A competition was devised using the analogy of ancient Egypt with a series of graphic and written clues to win a holiday in Egypt for two. The prominent window displays, posters and point-of-sale attracted thousands of potential new customers into the branches.

# Dillons Window Display

**CLIENT:** Pentos Retailing Ltd, Birmingham, UK

**DESIGNER:** Stocks Taylor Benson Ltd, Endersby, Leicestershire

**ILLUSTRATOR OR PHOTOGRAPHER:** Copyright-free images

**DATE OF COMPLETION:** February 1991

**TARGET MARKET:** ABC male/female, equal bias; 25–60 years old

**PLACE OF SALE:** Dillons the Bookstore and Athena Bookstores (approximately 100 outlets)

**CLIENT'S BRIEF:** To create a more theatrical and three-dimensional set of window display material that would be interchangeable throughout the spring season.

**DESIGN RATIONALE:** Great flexibility of items meant that card 'props' could be interchangeable and therefore maintain freshness. Columns and urns give a feel that is traditional and upmarket.

EASTER

## Fuzzy Peach

**CLIENT:** Body Shop, London, UK

**DESCRIPTION OF PRODUCT:** Range of peach-scented products (perfume, soaps, etc.)

**DESIGNER:** Alan McDougall and Frances Myers, Body Shop

**ILLUSTRATOR OR PHOTOGRAPHER:** Tom Connell

**DATE OF COMPLETION:** January 1991

**TARGET MARKET:** Female, all ages

**PLACE OF SALE:** Window and in-store Body Shops

## Who Do We Think We Are 'Millenium'

**CLIENT:** Body Shop, London, UK

**DESCRIPTION OF PRODUCT:** Anthropological book and TV series

**DESIGNER:** Frances Myers, Body Shop

**ILLUSTRATOR OR PHOTOGRAPHER:** Carol Beckwith

**DATE OF COMPLETION:** April 1992

**TARGET MARKET:** Male/female, all ages

**PLACE OF SALE:** Window and in-store promotion

**DESIGN RATIONALE:** To raise awareness of the plight of indigenous peoples around the world. To celebrate the diversity of cultures and what we can learn from them.

## Where do loofahs really come from?

**CLIENT:** Body Shop, London, UK

**DESCRIPTION OF PRODUCT:** All Body Shop suncare products and sundry items

**DESIGNER:** Frances Myers, Body Shop

**ILLUSTRATOR OR PHOTOGRAPHER:** Christopher Corr

**DATE OF COMPLETION:** April 1991

**TARGET MARKET:** Male/female, all ages

**PLACE OF SALE:** Window and in-store Body Shops

## Colour Tints

**CLIENT:** Body Shop, London, UK

**DESCRIPTION OF PRODUCT:** Lipsticks

**DESIGNER:** Frances Myers, Body Shop

**ILLUSTRATOR OR PHOTOGRAPHER:** Frances Myers

**DATE OF COMPLETION:** February 1991

**TARGET MARKET:** Female, all ages

**PLACE OF SALE:** Window and in-store Body Shops

## Cool Clean Cucumber

**CLIENT:** Body Shop, London, UK

**DESCRIPTION OF PRODUCT:** Cucumber cleanser and skin toner

**DESIGNER:** Frances Myers, Richard Browning, Debbie Littley, Body Shop

**ILLUSTRATOR OR PHOTOGRAPHER:** Tom Connell

**DATE OF COMPLETION:** February 1991

**TARGET MARKET:** Females/males, all ages

**PLACE OF SALE:** Window and in-store Body Shops

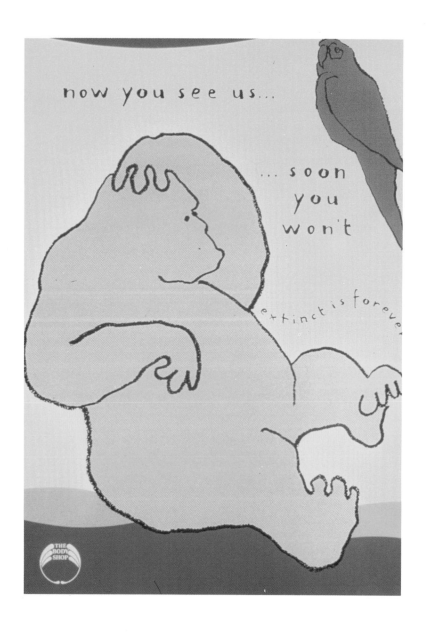

## Extinct is Forever

**CLIENT:** Body Shop, London, UK

**DESCRIPTION OF PRODUCT:** Soaps and sundry items that heighten awareness that animals face extinction

**DESIGNER:** Frances Myers and Bertha Thackeray, Body Shop

**ILLUSTRATOR OR PHOTOGRAPHER:** Frances Myers

**DATE OF COMPLETION:** March 1992

**TARGET MARKET:** Primarily children and young adults

**PLACE OF SALE:** Window and in-store Body Shops

**DESIGN RATIONALE:** To raise awareness of plight of rare animals which are in danger of extinction. To promote range of products, especially among children, and encourage them to take action to help preserve animals in danger.

## Complete Colour

**CLIENT:** Body Shop, London, UK

**DESCRIPTION OF PRODUCT:** Cosmetics that can be used to colour eyes, lips and cheeks

**DESIGNER:** Frances Myers, Body Shop

**ILLUSTRATOR OR PHOTOGRAPHER:** Ivan Alen

**DATE OF COMPLETION:** March 1992

**TARGET MARKET:** Female, all ages

**PLACE OF SALE:** Window and in-store Body Shops

## Colour Correctives

**CLIENT:** Body Shop, London, UK

**DESCRIPTION OF PRODUCT:** Make-up to help disguise discoloured skin/birthmarks, etc.

**DESIGNER:** Frances Myers and Fionnuala Conway, Body Shop

**ILLUSTRATOR OR PHOTOGRAPHER:** Frances Myers

**DATE OF COMPLETION:** September 1991

**TARGET MARKET:** Male/female, all ages

**PLACE OF SALE:** Window and in-store Body Shops

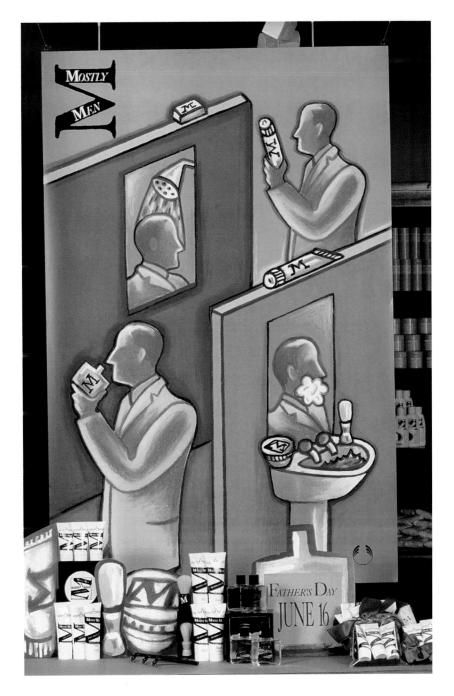

## Mostly Men

**CLIENT:** Body Shop, London, UK

**DESCRIPTION OF PRODUCT:** Male cleansing, shaving and bath products

**DESIGNER:** Frances Myers

**ILLUSTRATOR OR PHOTOGRAPHER:** Richard Spice

**TARGET MARKET:** Males, all ages

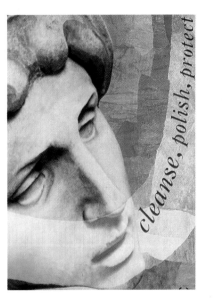

## Cleanse, Polish, Protect Face

**CLIENT:** Body Shop, London, UK

**DESCRIPTION OF PRODUCT:** All Body Shop skincare products

**DESIGNER:** Alison Philpot, Body Shop

**ILLUSTRATOR OR PHOTOGRAPHER:** Alison Philpot

**DATE OF COMPLETION:** December 1991

**TARGET MARKET:** Male/female, all ages

**PLACE OF SALE:** Window and in-store Body Shops

## Poster Series

**CLIENT:** Decca Record Company, London, UK

**DESCRIPTION OF PRODUCT:** Posters

**DESIGNER:** The Partners, London, UK

**ILLUSTRATOR OR PHOTOGRAPHER:** Various

**DATE OF COMPLETION:** January 1989

**TARGET MARKET:** Retail

**PLACE OF SALE:** Record shops

**CLIENT'S BRIEF:** Posters were to be part of a scheme to encompass the wide range of products that Decca sells.

**DESIGN RATIONALE:** The Partners took a disciplined approach to design in which strictly ordered typography and consistent visual elements made all posters, brochures and adverts instantly recognizable. For the posters, imagery was built up in layers to create visual excitement.

sir georg solti    DECCA

## Wilkes Bashford Spring '89 Visual Identity

**CLIENT:** Wilkes Bashford, San Francisco, California, USA

**DESIGNER:** Morla Design Inc, San Francisco, California, USA

**ILLUSTRATOR OR PHOTOGRAPHER:** Jennifer Morla

**DATE OF COMPLETION:** January 1989

**TARGET MARKET:** High-end men's fashion

**PLACE OF SALE:** Wilkes Bashford Department Stores, USA

**DESIGN RATIONALE:** For high-end men's fashion boutique. Leger-inspired illustration allowed for proper positioning of the varied Spring clothing line.

## Armani Glasses

**CLIENT:** Giorgio Armani, Italy

**DESCRIPTION OF PRODUCT:** Acetate covered slip-case with photograph of glasses

**DESIGNER:** Maddie Bennett, London, UK

**DATE OF COMPLETION:** June 1989

**TARGET MARKET:** International market

**PLACE OF SALE:** Worldwide distribution

**CLIENT'S BRIEF:** To produce an international house style for Giorgio Armani glasses. The photographic image and simple typography combine to create a distinctive brand identity, endorsed with the quality of Armani.

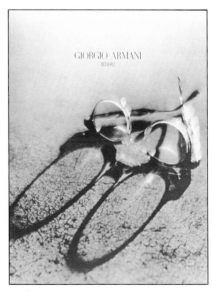

## Dillons Christmas Display

**CLIENT:** Pentos Retailing Ltd, Birmingham

**DESIGNER:** Stocks Taylor Benson Ltd, Enderby, Leicestershire

**ILLUSTRATOR/PHOTOGRAPHER:** Stocks Taylor Benson Ltd

**DATE OF COMPLETION:** November 1990

**TARGET MARKET:** ABC male/female equal bias; 25–60 years old

**PLACE OF SALE:** Dillons The Bookstore and Athena Bookstores (approximately 100 outlets)

**CLIENT'S BRIEF:** To create attractive seasonal point of purchase, primarily for windows, that could be carried through in-store.

**DESIGN RATIONALE:** A high-impact clown character was used to link all items by style and colour to create colourful yet traditional and sophisticated display graphics, appropriate to the target market.

## Peter Rabbit

**CLIENT:** Frederick Warne, Penguin Books, London, UK

**DESCRIPTION OF PRODUCT:** Cardboard cut-out, free-standing display piece (45 × 32cm)

**DESIGNER:** Frederick Warne, Penguin Books, London, UK

**DATE OF COMPLETION:** 1985

**TARGET MARKET:** Booktrade

**PLACE OF SALE:** Bookshops

**CLIENT'S BRIEF:** To design an eye-catching free-standing point-of-purchase display piece using Beatrix Potter's *Peter Rabbit* character, incorporating a novelty element and remaining true to Beatrix Potter's original illustrations and style.

**DESIGN RATIONALE:** An interactive novelty style showcard was produced that enables Peter Rabbit to pop out of the watering can.

## The Tailor Mouse

**CLIENT:** Frederick Warne, Penguin Books, London, UK

**DESCRIPTION OF PRODUCT:** Cardboard cut-out, free-standing display piece (45 × 32cm)

**DESIGNER:** Frederick Warne, Penguin Books, London, UK

**DATE OF COMPLETION:** 1985

**TARGET MARKET:** Booktrade

**PLACE OF SALE:** Bookshops

**CLIENT'S BRIEF:** To design a visually appealing free-standing display piece using Beatrix Potter's character *The Tailor Mouse*. It was important to remain true to the original illustration and style, and incorporate space for the display of a book.

**DESIGN RATIONALE:** An attractive showcard was produced using a cut-out of The Tailor Mouse. The book slot was positioned to look as though the character is holding the book, which is visually appealing and meets the requirements set out in the brief.

## The Quad Hi-Fi Product Range

**CLIENT:** Quad Electro-acoustics Limited, Huntingdon, Cambridgeshire, UK

**DESIGNER:** Dinah Lone, RSCG Conran Design, London, UK

**ILLUSTRATOR:** Helen Manning

**DATE OF COMPLETION:** June 1991

**TARGET MARKET:** Music lovers

**PLACE OF SALE:** Independent hi-fi retailers and department stores

**CLIENT'S BRIEF:** To get the customer to focus on Quad products displayed alongside competitors' products either in the window or instore. The graphic display must work with stacked groups and individual products. It must be recognized as Quad without identifying individual products. An inexpensive, simple, high-quality solution, stressing the relationship with Quad and music.

**DESIGN RATIONALE:** Three display headers, two for positioning on top of the product and one behind, creating a 3-dimensional stepped effect. Each header comprises a single sheet of card, die-cut and scored. Delivered flat, they are simple to construct. Creative illustration depicting stylized musical performance is an integral part of the cut-out, folding design.

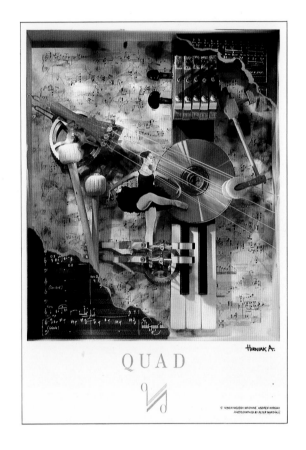

## The Quad Hi-Fi Product Range

**CLIENT:** Quad Electro-acoustics Limited, Huntingdon, Cambridgeshire, UK

**DESIGNER:** Dinah Lone, RSCG Conran Design, London, UK

**ILLUSTRATORS:** Paul Wearing, Andrew Hirniak

**DATE OF COMPLETION:** The last poster was printed in November 1990. This is an on-going project with new posters commissioned when budgets allow

**TARGET MARKET:** Mainly serious music lovers, also hi-fi enthusiasts

**PLACE OF SALE:** Independent hi-fi retailers and department stores

**CLIENT'S BRIEF:** To identify a 'Quad' area primarily within listening rooms. Also for use in window displays and exhibition stands. An inexpensive, high-quality solution which must work within a wide range of standards of interiors and situations and be implemented by the retailer with no guidelines.

**DESIGN RATIONALE:** A2 format posters with a consistent layout combining the image area and the Quad identity in a set of 'Fine Art' posters. The use of highly creative and diverse imagery directly inspired by different types of music, such as opera, jazz and classical, to appeal to the serious music lover.

## Theme Poster

**CLIENT:** Thresher Wine Shops, Welwyn Garden City, Herts, UK

**DESCRIPTION OF PRODUCT:** Theme poster paper/screen printing 30in × 40in

**DESIGNER:** Hanneka Steenmetz, Nucleus Design, Thames Ditton, Surrey, UK

**ILLUSTRATOR:** Lawrence Zeegan

**DATE OF COMPLETION:** January 1991

**TARGET MARKET:** Thresher customers

**PLACE OF SALE:** Thresher Wine Stores

**CLIENT'S BRIEF:** To design a range of point-of-purchase material to promote a 'sale' in which shop managers would be able to promote individual products.

**DESIGN RATIONALE:** The theme 'Wrap Up a Winter Bargain' was developed to communicate the special offer message. This was then interpreted in a bold, graphic and distinctive way, combining informal illustration with striking colours.

## Theme Poster

**CLIENT:** Thresher Wine Shops, Welwyn Garden City, Herts, UK

**DESCRIPTION OF PRODUCT:** Theme poster paper/screen printing 30in × 40in

**DESIGNER:** Troy Litten, Nucleus Design, Thames Ditton, Surrey, UK

**ILLUSTRATOR:** In-house

**DATE OF COMPLETION:** March 1991

**TARGET MARKET:** Wine customers

**PLACE OF SALE:** Thresher Wine Stores

**CLIENT'S BRIEF:** To create a visual theme to assist in promoting a new range of 40 Southern France wines.

**DESIGN RATIONALE:** The title 'The Beautiful South' was created to give the promotion a memorable theme. Designs were created that combined an impactful graphic 'icon' with a bold, but appropriate, use of colour.

## BHS Fashion Themes

**CLIENT:** British Home Stores, London, UK

**DESIGNER:** James Pyott, London, UK

**LAUNCH DATE:** 1989

**PLACE OF SALE:** British Home Stores retail outlets

**CLIENT'S BRIEF:** Point-of-purchase for in-store promotion of fashion themes. The design had to promote and show off mannequins which stood in front of the banners.

## BHS Price Reduction

**CLIENT:** British Home Stores, London, UK

**DESIGNER:** James Pyott, London, UK

**LAUNCH DATE:** 1989

**PLACE OF SALE:** British Home Stores retail outlets

**CLIENT'S BRIEF:** To produce a strong and aggressive campaign to announce a reduction in prices owing to refurbishment.

## BHS Summer Fashions

**CLIENT:** British Home Stores, London, UK

**DESIGNER:** James Pyott, London, UK

**LAUNCH DATE:** 1989

**PLACE OF SALE:** British Home Stores retail outlets

**CLIENT'S BRIEF:** Summer shop was designed to promote summer fashions within the store to generally make the shop feel exciting. Also it had to act as a backdrop to display the clothes.

### Polaroid Promotion

**CLIENT:** Polaroid Corporation, London, UK

**DESCRIPTION OF PRODUCT:** Business and professional packaging, point-of-purchase and promotional material

**DESIGNER:** John Rushworth, Bob Mytton, Pentagram Design Ltd, London, UK

**DATE OF COMPLETION:** 1989

**CLIENT'S BRIEF:** Speed, confidentiality and accuracy make Polaroid instant film valuable for business and professional use, and as an effective means of communication. New packaging, point-of-purchase and promotional material was designed to promote this aspect of Polaroid.

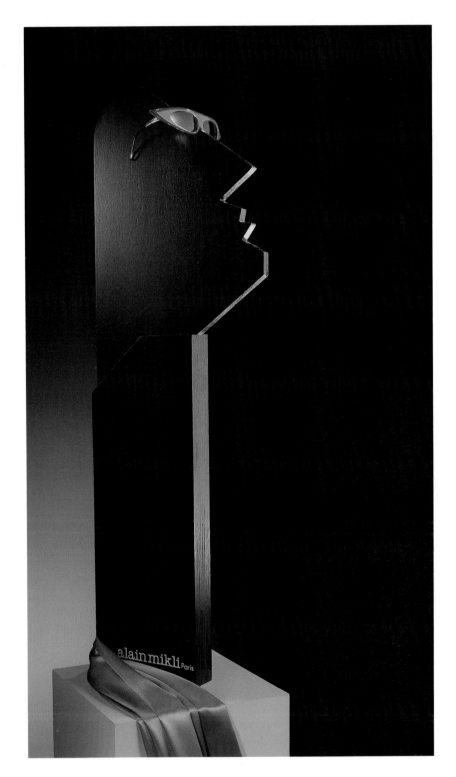

## Alain Mikli Glasses

**CLIENT:** Alain Mikli, Paris, France

**DESCRIPTION OF PRODUCT:** Wood silhouette display stand

**DESIGNER:** Pat PLV, Puteaux, France

**DATE OF COMPLETION:** 1987

**PLACE OF SALE:** Opticians

## Athletics Equipment

**CLIENT:** Champs Sports, New York, USA

**DESCRIPTION OF PRODUCT:** 18pt board for mannequin heads

**DESIGNER:** Medallion Associates, New York, USA

**DATE OF COMPLETION:** February 1992

**TARGET MARKET:** Primarily males aged 13–19, but also males aged 19–26

**PLACE OF SALE:** Champs Sports (athletic footwear, apparel and equipment retailer)

**CLIENT'S BRIEF:** To design a window display that would promote a specific theme.

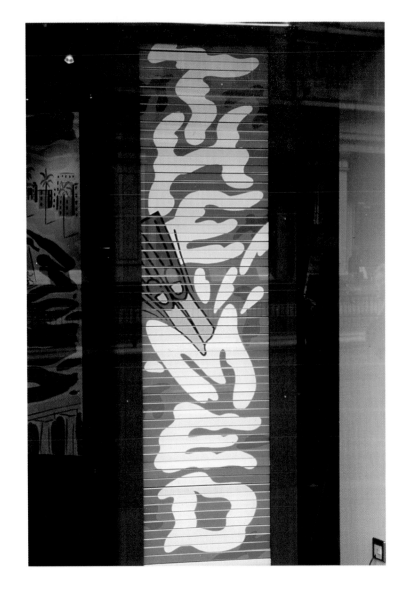

## Four Corners

**CLIENT:** Leagus Delaney, London, UK

**DESCRIPTION OF PRODUCT:** Silk screen panels

**DESIGNER:** The Partners, London, UK

**ILLUSTRATOR OR PHOTOGRAPHER:** 'British Breaks' Panel: Geoffrey Appleton; 'Great Trains' Panel: Line + Line; 'Planes' Panel: Malcolm English

**DATE OF COMPLETION:** April 1989

**TARGET MARKET:** Retail

**PLACE OF SALE:** Four Corners travel agents – window display

**CLIENT'S BRIEF:** To get over to the public that Four Corners was a travel agent; rotographic panels were to be used as part of different promotions within the store.

**DESIGN RATIONALE:** The design was constrained by having to use existing rotographic panels. It was decided to concentrate on the word of the theme and to make the word as lively, large and visually exciting as possible to draw people into the shop.

## Signage to Advertise
## Retail Space

**CLIENT:** SC Properties, London, UK

**DESIGNER:** The Partners, London, UK

**ILLUSTRATOR OR PHOTOGRAPHER:** Mathew Weinreb

**SIGN MANUFACTURE:** Jon Goodwin

**DATE OF COMPLETION:** November/December 1991

**TARGET MARKET:** International retailers

**PLACE OF SALE:** Corner building of Piccadilly and Old
Bond Street – shop window

**CLIENT'S BRIEF:** A window display for the large retail site
on the corner of Piccadilly and Old Bond Street, which
would attract international retailers.

**DESIGN RATIONALE:** The display takes the form of a
giant surveyor's tape running the entire length of the
shop front (approximately 45m/140ft).

## Store Promotion – Christmas

**CLIENT:** Paperchase, London, UK

**DESCRIPTION OF PRODUCT:** From small tree decorations on card to 7' × 3' window displays on board

**DESIGNER:** Janine Hall/Chris Keeble, Keeble & Hall, London, UK

**ILLUSTRATOR:** Boy & Horse: Graham Philpot; Special lettering: Alan Dempsey

**DATE OF COMPLETION:** Autumn 1989

**TARGET MARKET:** Christmas shoppers

**PLACE OF SALE:** Paperchase: specialist paper and giftstores

**CLIENT'S BRIEF:** To create a traditional warm Victorian Christmas theme capable of working on carrier bags, point-of-purchase window displays, product packaging, in-store siting.

**DESIGN RATIONALE:** To take the client's brief and translate it into graphics – the central element is redrawn from an old Victorian engraving of a boy on a rocking horse (which is now produced in colour) which is supported by special hand-drawn lettering and a green colour theme

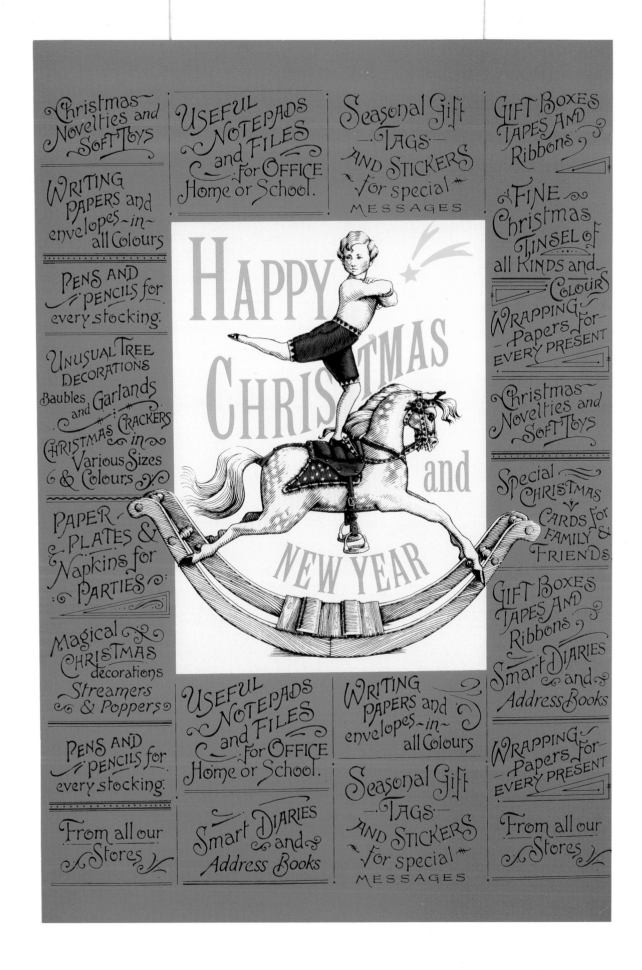

Christmas Novelties and Soft Toys

WRITING PAPERS and envelopes ~in~ all Colours

PENS AND PENCILS for every stocking.

UNUSUAL TREE DECORATIONS Baubles and Garlands CHRISTMAS CRACKERS in Various Sizes & Colours

PAPER PLATES & Napkins for PARTIES

Magical CHRISTMAS decorations Streamers & Poppers

PENS AND PENCILS for every stocking.

From all our Stores

USEFUL NOTEPADS and FILES for OFFICE Home or School.

USEFUL NOTEPADS and FILES for OFFICE Home or School.

Smart DIARIES and Address Books

Seasonal Gift TAGS AND STICKERS for special MESSAGES

WRITING PAPERS and envelopes ~in~ all Colours

Seasonal Gift TAGS AND STICKERS for special MESSAGES

GIFT BOXES TAPES AND Ribbons

FINE Christmas TINSEL of all KINDS and COLOURS

WRAPPING Papers for EVERY PRESENT

Christmas Novelties and Soft Toys

Special CHRISTMAS CARDS for FAMILY & FRIENDS.

GIFT BOXES TAPES AND Ribbons

Smart DIARIES and Address Books

WRAPPING Papers for EVERY PRESENT

From all our Stores

HAPPY CHRISTMAS and NEW YEAR

49

Hanging cards (above) and carrier bags (opposite) – part
of the Paperchase Christmas display material designed by
Keeble and Hall. See also pp 48–9.

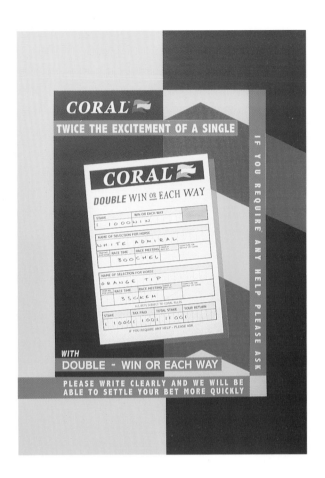

## Coral Betting Shop

**CLIENT:** Coral, Barking, Essex, UK

**DESCRIPTION OF PRODUCT:** Window graphics to promote betting shops

**DESIGNER:** Brem Bremner & Russ O'Donnell, Light & Coley Ltd, London, UK

**ILLUSTRATOR OR PHOTOGRAPHER:** Chris Dreja

**DATE OF COMPLETION:** Spring 1992

**TARGET MARKET:** Existing and potential new consumers

**PLACE OF SALE:** Betting shop services on the high street

**CLIENT'S BRIEF:** To develop point-of-purchase for the betting shop windows that would create excitement and appeal to both existing and potential customers. The images could not be accompanied with any words and had to break the mould of traditional, clichéd horse racing imagery.

**DESIGN RATIONALE:** Light & Coley developed images that both pulled the observer into the action and conversely projected the action into the high street. The designs communicated sporting excitement in the broadest sense and endorsed the overall Coral plan of broadening the appeal of the betting shop both in terms of the product on offer and to a wider audience.

## Sony Mini Hi-Fi System

**CLIENT:** Sony UK Ltd, Staines, Middlesex, UK

**DESCRIPTION OF PRODUCT:** Three-piece portable mini
hi-fi system (upright) 225 × 370 × 275mm; speakers
(each) 185 × 115 × 225mm

**DESIGNER:** Martin Smith, Clarke Hooper Consulting,
Slough, Berkshire, UK

**ILLUSTRATOR OR PHOTOGRAPHER:** Andy Holmes

**DATE OF COMPLETION:** 1988

**TARGET MARKET:** Under-35s: affluent and mobile

**PLACE OF SALE:** Sony centres, independent Sony
stockists and high street electrical multiples.

**CLIENT'S BRIEF:** The Sony new mini hi-fi system was the
first hi-fi system to offer consumers true 'portability'. The
brief from Sony was to produce innovative, eye-catching
generic point-of-purchase aimed at the younger,
affluent, 80s 'yuppie' market.

**DESIGN RATIONALE:** Some humour was needed to
differentiate Sony black boxes, together with a very
stylized graphic approach that would appeal to the
target market and ensure the product and point-of-
purchase stood out in-store.

## Oddbins Posters

**CLIENT:** Oddbins, London, UK

**DESIGNER:** Miller & Leeves, London, UK

Spanish porter : Retail Advertising Services, London, UK

**ILLUSTRATOR:** Ralph Steadman

**DATE OF COMPLETION:** 1989–1992

**TARGET MARKET:** Wine drinkers of all ages

**PLACE OF SALE:** Off licences

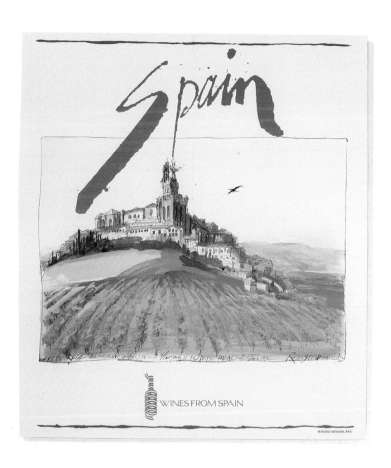

**Floor-standing units** Most supermarket chains and large-scale retail outlets have their share of floor-standing merchanizers, dump bins, "gondolas" and dispensers. They are often situated at the end of an aisle or a run of units, and manufacturers launching a new product or brand – coordinated with a burst of advertising – will negotiate (and often pay for) space to put in their own construction. These have the advantage of isolating the product from its competitors, and displaying, in a controlled environment, a larger quantity of the product than might otherwise be possible.

Some products, like sunglasses, look much better when displayed on specially designed fittings that retailers cannot provide or do not have shelf space for. Some products, like cars, are often sold in spaces where no display facilities or wall fittings are provided. Some products, like tapes and CDs, sell better when demonstration facilities are provided. And when these facilities, these units, these fittings, look attractive, stylish and well-designed, the products move that much quicker.

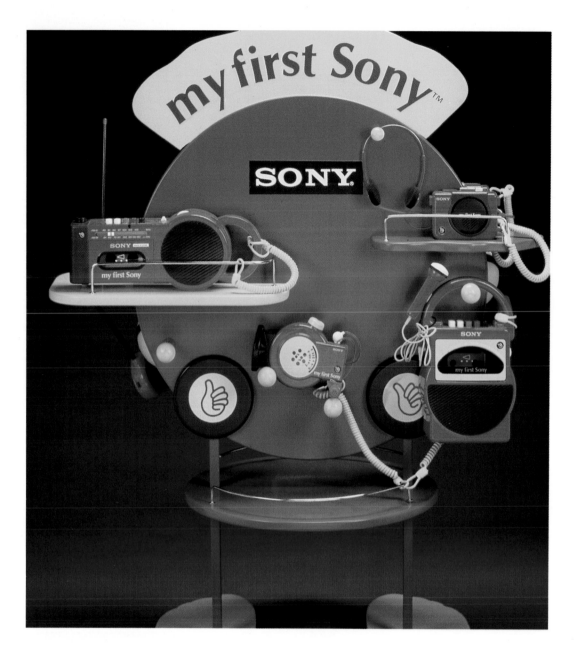

## My First Sony Floor-Standing Merchandizer

**CLIENT:** Sony UK Ltd, Staines, Middlesex, UK

**DESCRIPTION OF PRODUCT:** Floor-standing
merchandizer. Size: Height 1260mm, Width 910mm,
Depth 580mm. Materials: medium-density fibreboard,
spray-finish non-toxic paint, screen-printed graphics.
Supplied as flat pack – retailer to construct

**DESIGNER:** Alan Taylor, Creative Director, Oakley Young
4th Dimension, Leicester, UK

**DATE OF COMPLETION:** 1991–1992 (on-going)

**TARGET MARKET:** Male and female (age 3–10 years) and
adult interest

**PLACE OF SALE:** Sony Centres UK, Sony Europe:
Switzerland/Denmark. Also UK independent electrical
retail outlets

**CLIENT'S BRIEF:** To increase awareness and therefore
sales of the My First Sony range. To convey an image of
quality, unique features, ease of use and safety,
targeting the younger persons introduction to audio
products.

**DESIGN RATIONALE:** The My First Sony bar was designed
to appeal not only to children but to adults, with all
products easily demonstrable to both through a bright
and attractive fun-packed floor merchandizer. Height
and scale were of major importance. The unit has no
sharp edges and is strong and stable. Security is
maintained through coloured cables which form part of
the display.

## My First Sony

**CLIENT:** Sony France, Paris, France

**DESCRIPTION OF PRODUCT:** Cardboard and sheet metal; size: height 2000mm; width 800mm; depth 800mm

**DESIGNER:** Prisme, Suresnes, France

**DATE OF COMPLETION:** June 1991

**TARGET MARKET:** Children

**PLACE OF SALE:** Sony's traditional point-of-purchase and toy shops.

**CLIENT'S BRIEF:** To create a permanent floor display to demonstrate the 17 products of the My First Sony line targeted for four- to ten-year-olds. The 17 products must be able to be used but not carried off. It also had to reflect that Sony's high technology and quality standards are not only for grown ups but also for children.

**DESIGN RATIONALE:** To answer these requirements the designers chose a square tower that a child could have built himself with sand or Lego. It was given the Sony look by using black lacquered sheet metal. The black matte background also emphasizes the bright colours of the products, the roof recalls these colours. The products are mounted on the side of the tower, the level of each product depending on the age of the user.

## Window Support for Make-up

**CLIENT:** Shiseido, Paris, France

**DESCRIPTION OF PRODUCT:** Cardboard and black Plexi

**DESIGNER:** Jean-Pierre Toth, Méthacryl, Paris, France

**DATE OF COMPLETION:** 1990

**PLACE OF SALE:** Department stores and perfumeries

**CLIENT'S BRIEF:** To respect the Shiseido identity and colour code (black and red); to use geometrical shapes.

## Battistoni Cigarettes

**CLIENT:** Philip Morris Europe SA, Lausanne, Switzerland

**DESCRIPTION OF PRODUCT:** Plexiglas;
size 60 × 60 × 200cm

**DESIGNER:** Maurice Progin, Lausanne, Switzerland

**ILLUSTRATOR OR PHOTOGRAPHER:** Horst Neuffer,
Lausanne, Switzerland

**DATE OF COMPLETION:** 1990

**TARGET MARKET:** Duty free customers

**PLACE OF SALE:** Tax-free world exhibition for launching
new product

**CLIENT'S BRIEF:** To make something attractive in
accordance with the marketing information and
brand image.

## Camcorder Demonstration Unit

**CLIENT:** JVC., London, UK

**DESCRIPTION OF UNIT:** Laminated MDF construction using electronic switching gear

**DESIGNER:** Paul Osborne, Buchanan Group, London, UK

**DATE OF COMPLETION:** 1991

**TARGET MARKET:** 25–50 age group

**PLACE OF SALE:** Brown goods retail outlets

**CLIENT'S BRIEF:** To demonstrate JVC's range of camcorders

**DESIGN RATIONALE:** To design a compact, secure unit that could demonstrate camcorders by using an electronic comparitor unit, and also display accessories.

## Camcorder Bar

**CLIENT:** Sharp Electronics, London, UK

**DESCRIPTION OF PRODUCT:** Metal laminated MDF construction using electronic switching equipment

**DESIGNER:** Paul Osborne, Buchanan Group, London, UK

**DATE OF COMPLETION:** 1990

**TARGET MARKET:** 25–50 age group

**PLACE OF SALE:** Brown goods retail outlets

**CLIENT'S BRIEF:** To design a camcorder unit to display a range of camcorders.

**DESIGN RATIONALE:** A compact camcorder unit that allows a "hands on", secure demonstration unit to give the customer the opportunity to use and compare the camcorders using an electronics switching system.

## Sony Video Camcorder

**CLIENT:** Sony UK Ltd, Staines, Middlesex, UK

**DESCRIPTION OF PRODUCT:** Floor-standing Video 8
Interactive Comparitor, demonstrating four Sony
camcorders with full home studio edit facility, also
demonstrating Video 8 Walkman/Promotional VCR to
main monitor. Electronic control system also securitized
the products by alarm with non-mains battery back-up.
Lockable accessories display cabinet for software. Size:
Height 2030mm, Width 1m, Depth 700mm

**DESIGNER:** Mr Alan Taylor, Creative Director, Oakley
Young 4th Dimension, Leicester, UK

**PHOTOGRAPHER:** Barry Goodwin

**DATE OF COMPLETION:** 1991–1992 (on-going)

**TARGET MARKET:** 18-plus

**PLACE OF SALE:** Sony Centres UK. Also UK independent
electrical retail outlets (approximately 800 in total)

**CLIENT'S BRIEF:** To increase Sony's 'in-store' share of
camcorder sales at selected independent dealers; to
develop product turn of camcorders at store levels
through effective hands-on; to obtain additional spaces
for Sony apart from current camcorder bars.

**DESIGN RATIONALE:** The unit is designed to allow the
customer to pick up the camcorders and try them – a
vital element in achieving consumer acceptance in the
rapidly changing camcorder market. The bar displays the
complete range of Video 8 products and accessories, and
enables the consumer to compare relevant features.

## Motorola

**CLIENT:** Motorola, Netherlands

**DESCRIPTION OF PRODUCT:** Display Unit for Motorola
telephones

**DESIGNER:** Alrec POS Design, Hillegorn, The Netherlands

## Puiforcat

**CLIENT:** Puiforcat, La Plaine Saint Denis, France

**DESCRIPTION OF PRODUCT:** Wood, glass and steel. Size: width 1100mm; height 1060mm; depth 750mm.

**DESIGNER:** Prisme, Suresnes, France

**DATE OF COMPLETION:** September 1990

**TARGET MARKET:** Higher class market

**PLACE OF SALE:** Retail

**CLIENT'S BRIEF:** Recently Puiforcat has become established in new point-of-purchase other than its own shops. This cabinet has been designed to convey the quality and the aesthetism of the make.

**DESIGN RATIONALE:** To respect the styles created by Jean Puiforcat the cabinet was given a '1930 type look'. The identification of the Puiforcat brand mark is provided firstly by the luminous Puiforcat logo on the drop leaves of the presentation tables and, secondly, by the design of the goblet which is a key element of the Puiforcat make. More subtly, the five fins of luminous glass on either side of the cabinet repeat an important decorative element of the stone frontage of the new Puiforcat boutique in Avenue Matignon, Paris.

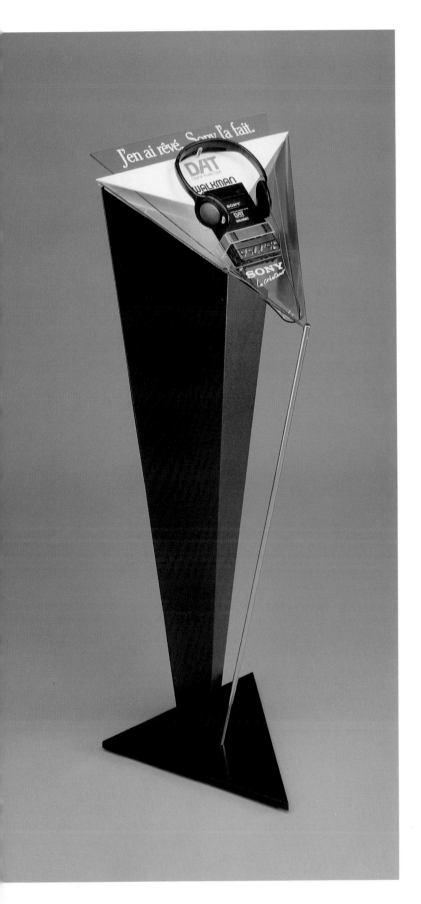

## Sony Dat Walkman

**CLIENT:** Sony France, Paris, France

**DESCRIPTION OF PRODUCT:** Laminated wood and lacquered sheet metal, acrylic vacuum-forming electric equipment. Size: height 1200mm; width 380mm; depth 420mm.

**DESIGNER:** Prisme, Suresnes, France

**DATE OF COMPLETION:** April 1991

**PLACE OF SALE:** Specialist hi-fi video stores

**CLIENT'S BRIEF:** To enhance the latest Sony creation: the digital audio tape Walkman, a unique product owing to its innovative and its highly technical nature in the market. To translate the technical nature of the product into the visual impact of the display stand, and to encourage the consumer to try the product on the spot.

**DESIGN RATIONALE:** To embody the idea of high technology, the stand incorporates the feeling of a sleek simple work of modern art. A sharp line in the design was chosen to emphasize the ultimate in technical advances. The Walkman is illuminated from below to evoke the light of genius and science. The Walkman is firmly attached to the stand while making it easy for the consumer to try it out.

## Honda Freestanding Display

**CLIENT:** Honda UK, London, UK

**DESCRIPTION OF PRODUCT:** Laminated MDF structure incorporating custom-designed LV lighting and cable system

**DESIGNER:** Paul Osborne, Buchanan Group, London, UK

**DATE OF COMPLETION:** 1990

**TARGET MARKET:** 30–50 age group

**PLACE OF SALE:** Honda dealerships

**CLIENT'S BRIEF:** To enhance the Honda environment and inject continuity into their dealerships nationwide.

**DESIGN rationale:** To use a classic column approach using LV lighting and lightboxes on a cable system to further promote the Honda range and serve to both enhance and punctuate the dealership environment.

## Jacques Dessange Make-up Stand

**CLIENT:** Jacques Dessange, Paris, France

**DESCRIPTION OF PRODUCT:** Presentation display piece for a range of make-up

**DESIGNER:** Jean-Réné Guegan, Ekonos, Paris, France

**DATE OF COMPLETION:** November 1989

**TARGET MARKET:** Clients of the Jacques Dessange hairdressing salons, and certain pharmacies

**CLIENT'S BRIEF:** To research and conceive a presentation display piece for an entire range of make up; it had to be coherent with the graphic image developed for the range of make-up.

**DESIGN RATIONALE:** The presentation of the whole range reflected the nuances of each range of products: face make-up, powder, lipstick, nail polish and mascara.

## Display for Solars of Stendhal

**CLIENT:** Sanofi Beauté, Paris, France

**DESCRIPTION OF PRODUCT:** This display is composed of garden furniture, including an armchair, a footstool and a tea trolley. All these elements piled up form the basic structure of the display. Backing form boxes carry the products. Dimensions: 180 × 40 × 40cm.

**DESIGNER:** RS Creation, Montreuil, France

**DATE OF COMPLETION:** 1987

**TARGET MARKET:** Top-end market

**PLACE OF SALE:** Specialized perfume shops and retailers

**CLIENT'S BRIEF:** To create a display table to stock sun-care products on rollers, easy to use and taking up little space, that reminded customers of the sun, and that the retailer could use afterwards.

**DESIGN RATIONALE:** The theme used is both playful and functional, the yellow canvas being reminiscent of sunshine. The re-usable aspect of the elements is an important factor for the retailer. A counter display was also distributed.

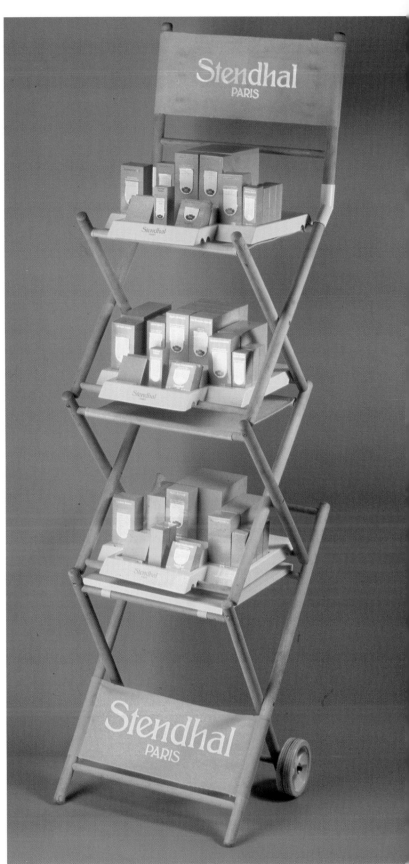

## Miele 'Black Diamond'

**CLIENT:** Miele France, Paris, France

**DESCRIPTION OF PRODUCT:** Vacuum cleaner

**DESIGNER:** Ateliers Reunis, Bagnolet, France

**DATE OF COMPLETION:** Summer 1990

**TARGET MARKET:** Most clients

**PLACE OF SALE:** Electrical goods retailers: 'Boulanger' group

**CLIENT'S BRIEF:** Miele France wanted a point-of-purchase display which characterized the anthracite grey metallic nature of the vacuum cleaner casing, as well as its compactness.

**DESIGN RATIONALE:** The idea was to create a display unit which was reminiscent of a wrapped present. The polystyrene mirror in the display showed, in five different angles, the image of the vacuum cleaner like the facets of a diamond – a reminder of its name – 'Black Diamond'. The coldness of the metal and the mirror were 'warmed' by the use of halogen lighting to catch the eye of customers.

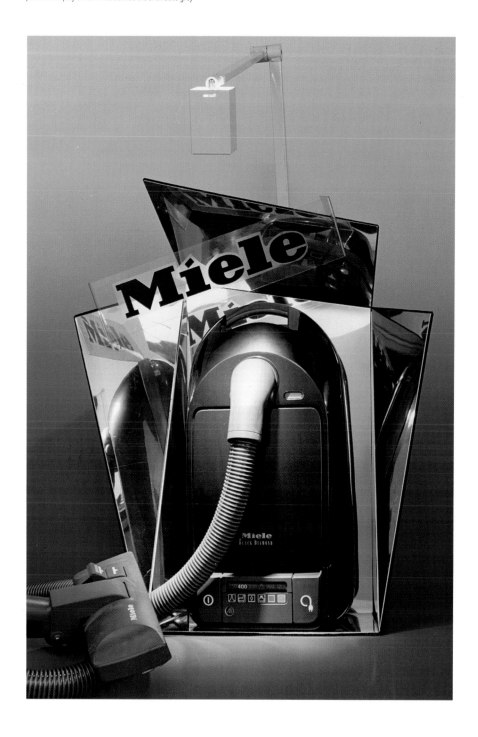

## Sarah Coventry Sunglasses

**CLIENT:** R. N. Koch, New York, USA

**DESCRIPTION OF PRODUCT:** Non-prescription fashion-frame sunglasses for females

**DESIGNER:** Barry David Berger & Associates, Inc, New York, USA

**TARGET MARKET:** Mid-level female market

**PLACE OF SALE:** Mid-level retailers

**CLIENT'S BRIEF:** To incorporate the following features: 160-frame capacity rotating fixture; modular construction for other potential quantities; high-style fixture to enhance frame style; flexible frame support location; group frames around three to four colour styles

**DESIGN RATIONALE:** The product layout insured against the homogeneous appearance of the product by orienting the frames in eight directions – four on a bridge support with 'temples' open, four on trays with 'temples' closed; the architectural appearance and neutral background colour enhanced the product styles and amplified the product colour palettes.

## Travelling Exhibition of Paloma Picasso

**CLIENT:** Prestige et Collections Internationale, Paris, France

**DESCRIPTION OF PRODUCT:** Safety glass and lacquered wood

**DESIGNER:** Prisme, Suresnes, France

**DATE OF COMPLETION:** June 1991

**TARGET MARKET:** Fashion-conscious and top end of the range purchasers – female

**PLACE OF SALE:** Department stores and European perfumeries

**CLIENT'S BRIEF:** To design a travelling exhibition stand that can be used in a space ranging from 5 to 20sq m in order to present the world of Paloma Picasso in different countries (Europe, USA, South America). The exhibition had to express Paloma Picasso's personality, not only through her perfume, make-up and bath lines, but also through her other creations: jewellery, leather goods, glasses, china.

**DESIGN RATIONALE:** Paloma Picasso's personality and image are very strong, her face and her colour have circled the globe. Her theatrical side is also a very important part of her image. A red curtain was the natural source of inspiration for the concept of this exhibit which links entertainment and identity. In order to show the objects and photos to their fullest advantage, three types of exhibition units were created using the same theme.

## Image Wall

**CLIENT:** Porsche Cars Great Britain Ltd, Reading, Berks, UK

**DESCRIPTION OF PRODUCT:** A series of 2m high modular panels manufactured from heat-formed foamex which can be configured in various combinations to form point-of-sale displays.

**DESIGNER:** John Furneaux, Furneaux Stewart Design & Communication, London, UK

**PHOTOGRAPHER:** Nicholas Gentilli

**DATE OF COMPLETION:** 1989

**TARGET MARKET:** Official Porsche Centre customers

**PLACE OF SALE:** Official Porsche Centre Network (dealership network) in Great Britain and worldwide

**DESIGN RATIONALE:** The brief called for a semi-permanent yet inherently flexible design solution. The system needed to be sufficiently permanent to ensure that the client's products, services and corporate identity were correctly and consistently displayed, yet flexible enough to perform as space divider or pure point-of sale system whenever required.

## Weiss Art Products Unit

**CLIENT:** Weiss Art, Sydney, Australia

**DESCRIPTION OF PRODUCT:** Extruded aluminium sections; vacuum-formed panels; timber shelving; 1m × 1m × 1m modules

**DESIGNER:** Design Field Pty Ltd, Paddington, NSW, Australia

**PHOTOGRAPHER:** Rob Little, Sydney, Australia

**TARGET MARKET:** Department stores and tourist retail outlets

**CLIENT'S BRIEF:** To design and prototype a point-of-purchase display for the exclusive range of Weiss fashion products, which include such diverse items as T-shirts, umbrellas, knitting kits, beach towels, sneakers and sweatshirts. Added to this was the requirement that the products could be sold in any number of countries.

**DESIGN RATIONALE:** The solution was a pack-flat, flexible display system, which, to avoid language and communication problems, used symbols to show the product and pattern, complementing the bold graphic style of the Weiss Art products themselves. The strong visual form of the structure allowed a wide range of products to be displayed homogeneously.

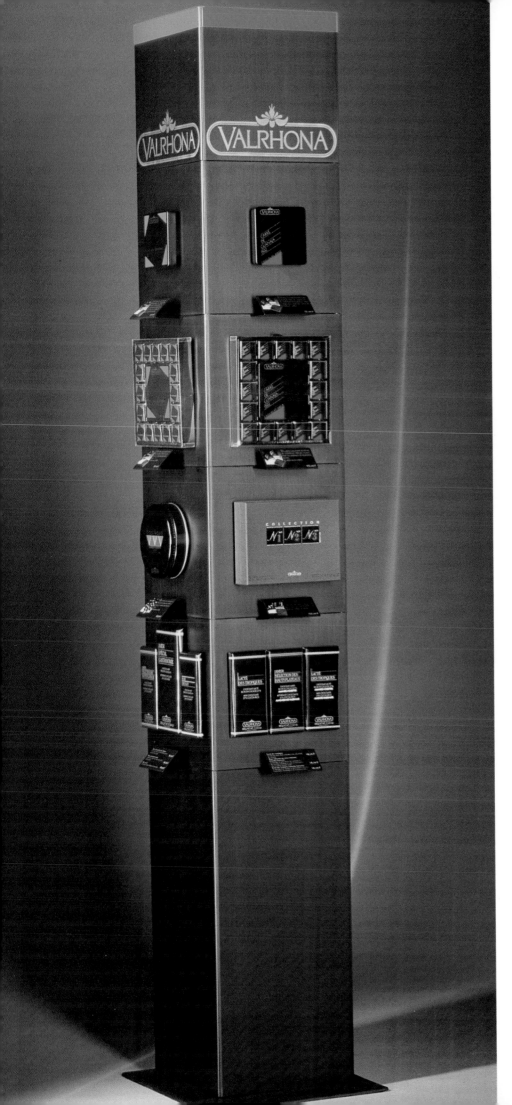

## L'espace Valrhona

**CLIENT:** Valrhona, Tain l'Hermitage, France

**DESCRIPTION OF PRODUCT:** Metal display stand presenting the whole range of Valrhona products. Height: 2m; width: 30cm

**DESIGNER:** MBD Design, Bagnolet Cedex, France

**DATE OF COMPLETION:** February 1992

**TARGET MARKET:** Baker's shops

**CLIENT'S BRIEF:** The stand display had to reinforce the brand and product image in baker's shops. The design work had to take into consideration the problem of space. Generally the retail outlets are very small.

**DESIGN RATIONALE:** MBD Design wanted to keep a strong image in line with the logo and the products. The proposition for the stand display was a square totem, presenting, keeping and distributing the whole range of Valrhona products.

The square can be found on the brand image and the "carrés" of Caraibes et Guanala. The impact comes from the height of the display stand although the constraint on the space is respected with its limited width.

# Listening Stand

**CLIENT:** Virgin Retail Ltd, London, UK

**DESIGNER:** 20/20 Design & Strategy Consultants, London, UK

**PHOTOGRAPHER:** Jon O'Brien

**DATE OF COMPLETION:** July 1990

**TARGET MARKET:** Music and video customers, 25–40 years

**PLACE OF SALE:** Virgin Megastores

**CLIENT'S BRIEF:** To make the Megastore the pre-eminent music outlet and to create a shopping environment that would be as exciting and adrenalin-pumping as the music itself. To expose customers to the full range of products available in the Megastore and to exploit these to maximum effect.

**DESIGN RATIONALE:** Prior to the development of the 'Listening Stand' customers could only listen to one record store-wide: that chosen by the store's DJ over the PA system. 20/20 developed the means by which customers could listen to and then buy some of the 60,000 music titles available in the Megastores. Having listened, the customer can pick up the product from the adjacent display and head for the cash till. The 'look' of the 'Listening Stand' was designed so as to blend with the rest of the 'Megastore' scheme.

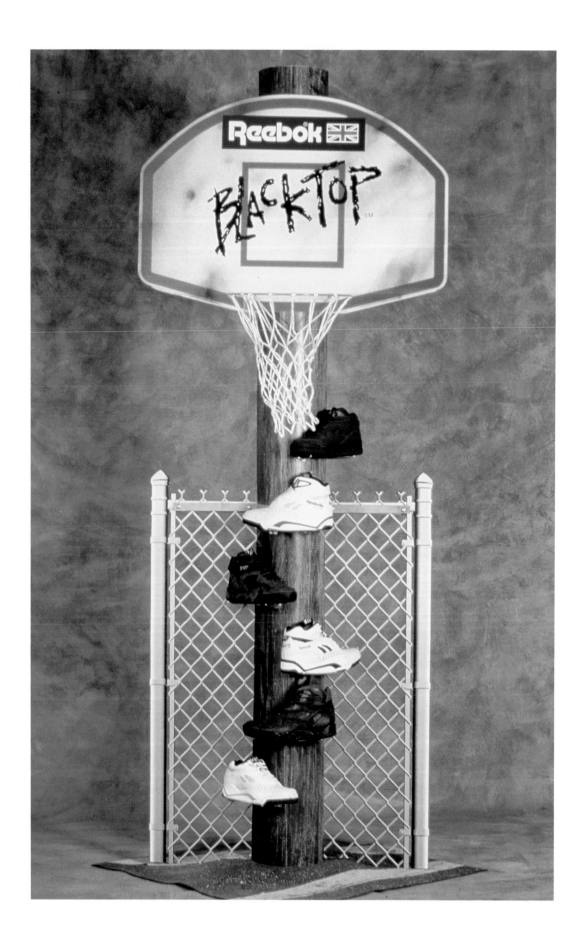

## Training Shoes

**CLIENT:** Footlocker/Reebok, Houghton, MA, USA

**DESCRIPTION OF PRODUCT:** Display stand

**DESIGNER:** Medallion Associates, New York, USA

**PLACE OF SALE:** Footlocker (Athletic Shoe Retailer), USA

**CLIENT'S BRIEF:** The 'Blacktop' display was designed specifically for basketball shoes and had to reflect the fact that the shoes are worn primarily on outdoor courts.

**Counter-top promotions** Anyone who has ever walked into the perfume department of a large department store will, once they have run the gauntlet of the sweet-talking demonstrators relentlessly spraying wrists with the latest scent, be aware of hundreds of immaculate little structures that cover every inch of the counter-top.

Having once worked on such structures, I am aware of the amount of time and care that is spent by the designers in trying to cram as creatively as possible the required number of lipsticks, blushers or eye-shadows into the smallest space, and at the same time present them in a new way that follows the advertising theme and includes the corporate logo and the fashion photography.

The examples I have chosen in this chapter seem to achieve these aims in effortless and inventive variety, and they also integrate the product in a considered and relevant way. But also included is a variety of other counter-top product categories from sunglasses and watches to trainers and jeans.

## React

**CLIENT:** Marks & Spencer PLC, London, UK

**DESIGNER:** Michael Sheridan & Co Ltd, Leicester, UK

**DATE OF COMPLETION:** 1989

**TARGET MARKET:** Men, middle/upper market, 16–45 years

**PLACE OF SALE:** Marks & Spencer retail outlets

**CLIENT'S BRIEF:** To provide a testing facility to support the launch of a new range of male toiletries to be sold within M&S outlets in UK, Europe and export markets. The design of the tester bar had to reflect the designer image of the pack design.

**DESIGN RATIONALE:** The size constraints were important to ensure siting on M&S shelves. Design, materials and finishes selected and specified had to appeal to the design-aware target market. Interchangeable product location had to be designed to accommodate future range additions or changes.

## Golden Beauty

**CLIENT:** Helena Rubenstein, Boulogne, France

**DESCRIPTION OF PRODUCT:** Display for Golden Beauty suncare products

**DESIGNER:** Raison Pure, Paris, France

**DATE OF COMPLETION:** March 1992

**TARGET MARKET:** Selective

**PLACE OF SALE:** Department stores and perfumeries

**CLIENT'S BRIEF:** To make a display for the launch of the Golden Beauty suncare line with a Tuscan, elegant, refined and luxurious backdrop.

**DESIGN RATIONALE:** To create a background for the product which conveys the image and the particular line in an imaginative way.

## **Rouge Forever Lipstick**

**CLIENT:** Helena Rubinstein, Boulogne, France

**DESCRIPTION OF PRODUCT:** Large stone wall with small niches for product

**DESIGNER:** Raison Pure, Paris, France

**DATE OF COMPLETION:** January 1992

**PLACE OF SALE:** Department stores and perfumeries

**CLIENT'S BRIEF:** To provide a window display for the Rouge Forever lipstick.

## Rapport

**CLIENT:** Shulton (GB) Ltd – (Debbie Rayner), Wokingham, Berkshire, UK

**DESCRIPTION OF PRODUCT:** Rapport merchandizer (counter-top pack-display stand)

**DESIGNER:** Kate Merrifield; Art Director: Julian Money, Pethick & Money, London, UK

**DATE OF COMPLETION:** September 1990

**TARGET MARKET:** 18–25 male

**PLACE OF SALE:** Chemists' shops

**CLIENT'S BRIEF:** To produce a merchandizer that can accommodate different types and combinations of product and sales promotion material.

**DESIGN RATIONALE:** To emulate the design of the bottle in the design of the merchandizer, through the use of subtle curvature and a matt black finish.

## No 7 Make-up Range

**CLIENT:** The Boots Company Ltd, Nottingham, UK

**DESCRIPTION OF PRODUCT:** Display stand

**DESIGNER:** KMD Marketing, Leicester, UK

**DATE OF COMPLETION:** 1992

**TARGET MARKET:** Female: mid-20s plus

**PLACE OF SALE:** Boots retail outlets

**CLIENT'S BRIEF:** To create a monthly promotion to introduce a new colour scheme for beauty products.

## Rose Cardin

**CLIENT:** Cardin, Paris, France

**DESCRIPTION OF PRODUCT:** Metal, plastic and textiles
display stand

**DESIGNER:** Pat PLV, Puteaux, France

**DATE OF COMPLETION:** October 1990

**PLACE OF SALE:** Perfumeries

## Shiseido Make-up Range

**CLIENT:** Shiseido, Paris, France

**DESCRIPTION OF PRODUCT:** Display units

**DESIGNER:** International Operations Division, Shiseido, Tokyo, Japan

**TARGET MARKET:** Women 25+

**PLACE OF SALE:** Department stores and pharmacies

## Carita

**CLIENT:** Carita, Paris, France

**DESIGNER:** PLV Services – MICAP, Noisy le Grand, France

**DATE OF COMPLETION:** 1992

**TARGET MARKET:** Women 25+

**PLACE OF SALE:** Perfumeries and department stores

**Shiseido**

**CLIENT:** Shiseido, Paris, France

**DESIGNER:** PLV Services – MICAP, Noisy le Grand, France

**DATE OF COMPLETION:** 1992

**TARGET MARKET:** Women 25+

**PLACE OF SALE:** Perfumeries and department stores

ténéré

paco rabanne

102

### Teneré; Calandre

**CLIENT:** Paco Rabanne, Paris, France
**DESIGNER:** PLV Services MICAP, Noisy le Grand, France
**DATE OF COMPLETION:** 1992
**TARGET MARKET:** Ténéré: men 25+;
Calandre: women 25+ .
**PLACE OF SALE:** Perfumeries and department stores

## Obsession Tester Counter Units

**CLIENT:** Calvin Klein Cosmetics, New York, USA

**DESCRIPTION OF PRODUCT:** Injection-moulded in polycarbonate, UV silkscreen for fragrance resistance; fabricated acrylic templates.

**DESIGNER:** Consumer Promotions, Inc, New York, USA

**DATE OF COMPLETION:** July 1990

**TARGET MARKET:** Female and male

**PLACE OF SALE:** Retail department stores

**CLIENT'S BRIEF:** The objective of this display programme was to develop a series of displays to present Obsession Men's and Obsession Women's testers, on counter. Four displays were required: Men's Deluxe, Men's Single Tester, Women's Deluxe, and Women's Single Tester. The design had to follow the lines of the product packaging, conveying a soft, sophisticated feeling. The materials used to manufacture these displays had to look first class, and the displays had to be of the highest quality.

**DESIGN RATIONALE:** The design of these displays reflects the styling of the primary packages, yielding soft and curved shapes. All units feature injection-moulded base and header, to provide a constant high-quality finish. Material compatability, often a problem with fragrances, was solved using a special polycarbonate resin, which is highly resistant to attack by fragrances while also providing a deep lustre and rich colour.

## Désirade

**CLIENT:** Parfums Aubusson, St Germain-en-Laye, France

**DESCRIPTION OF PRODUCT:** Plastic display stand

**DESIGNER:** Pat PLV, Puteaux, France

**DATE OF COMPLETION:** Beginning of 1991

**PLACE OF SALE:** Perfumeries

## Ombre Subtile
## Eyeshadow

**CLIENT:** Lancôme, Paris, France

**DESCRIPTION OF PRODUCT:** Display and tester unit, principally manufactured from injection-moulded polystyrene. Size: 43cm × 42cm × 26cm

**DESIGNER:** Studio DM Design, Paris and Creative Unit of Lancôme International Merchandizing

**DATE OF COMPLETION:** Spring 1992

**TARGET MARKET:** Female – sophisticated users of colour cosmetics

**PLACE OF SALE:** Department stores and perfumeries

**CLIENT'S BRIEF:** To create a display and tester unit for two new ranges of eyeshadows. They had to reflect the refinement of the product; feature the advertising visual for the product; show the new compact and test both ranges of product; the product testers had to be easily renewable.

**DESIGN RATIONALE:** To feature the existing Lancôme make-up corporate shades and colour for merchandizing.

## Display Stands for Lancôme

**CLIENT:** Lancôme, Paris, France

**DESCRIPTION OF PRODUCT:** Display stands and tester units for range of Lancôme products

**DESIGNER:** Studio DM Design, Paris and Creative Unit of Lancôme International Marketing

**DATE OF COMPLETION:** 1992

**TARGET MARKET:** Sophisticated panels

**PLACE OF SALE:** Department stores and perfumeries

## Trucco Cosmetics

**CLIENT:** Sebastian, Woodland Hills, California, USA

**DESCRIPTION OF PRODUCT:** Trucco Cosmetic point-of-purchase display is constructed from fabricated acrylic and a vacuum-formed tray/insert. Size: 16in × 14in × 2in

**DESIGNER:** Stuart Karten Design, Marina del Rey, California, USA

**ILLUSTRATOR OR PHOTOGRAPHER:** Henry Blackham

**DATE OF COMPLETION:** 1988

**TARGET MARKET:** Females aged 19 to 65

**PLACE OF SALE:** Professional hair salons

**CLIENT'S BRIEF:** The client needed a counter-top point-of-purchase that could easily be changed every four months. It needed to draw attention to the product line and to excite the customer.

**DESIGN RATIONALE:** A simple black acrylic display was created that accepts a black vacuum-formed insert. The insert changed every four months as new colours and products were highlighted. It needed to be easy to replace. The insert design and form had to change with each new introduction. The forms would be representational of the concept for that season (in other words natural colors would be represented with natural forms, water, stone etc.).

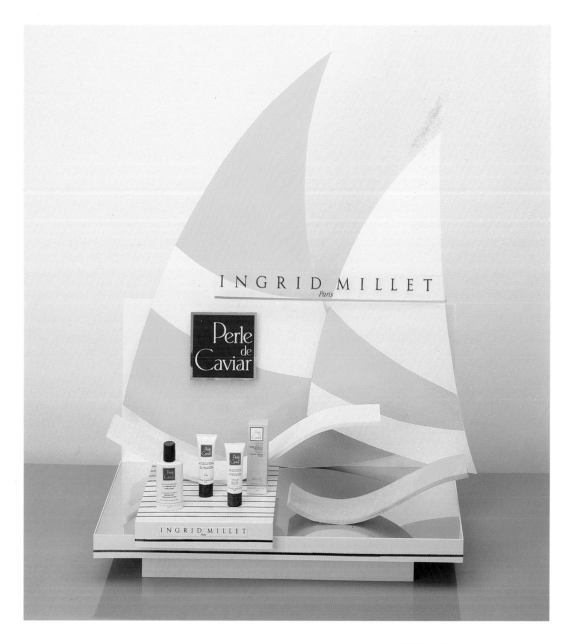

## Ingrid Millet Shop Window Display

**CLIENT:** Ingrid Millet/Groupe
Revillon, Paris, France

**DESCRIPTION OF PRODUCT:** Display, 1 × 2m

**DESIGNER:** Jean-Pierre Toth, Méthacryl, Paris, France

**DATE OF COMPLETION:** 1989

**PLACE OF SALE:** Ingrid Millet authorized shops

**CLIENT'S BRIEF:** To promote solar products of the Perle de Caviar range, and to evoke the sea, sun and water.

**DESIGN RATIONALE:** Atmosphere of the sea and sun represented by the sails of the stylized deckchair with white and yellow as predominant colours.

## Ingrid Millet Product Support

**CLIENT:** Ingrid Millet/Groupe Revillon, Paris, France

**DESIGNER:** Jean-Pierre Toth, Méthacryl, Suresnes, France

**DATE OF COMPLETION:** 1990

**PLACE OF SALE:** Ingrid Millet shops

**CLIENT'S BRIEF:** To promote a range of products – Nature Active luxury beauty products – to recreate the atmosphere of a beauty institute: clean and sober.

**DESIGN RATIONALE:** To recreate the atmosphere of a beauty institute in-store and a situation for a luxury product

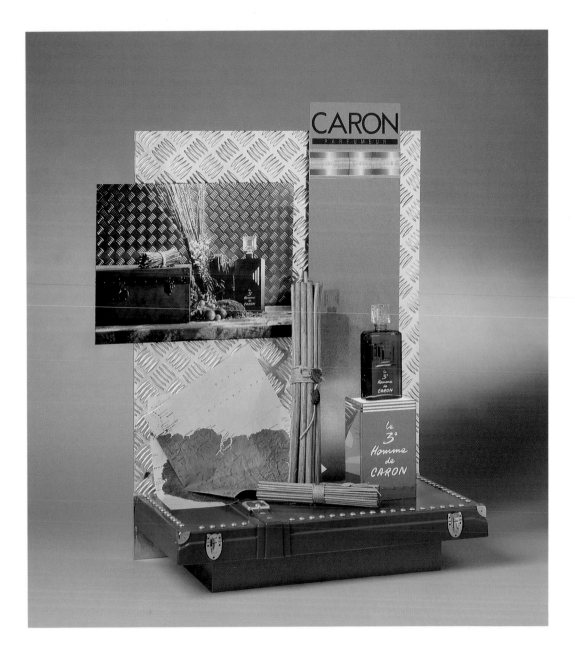

## Window Visual Support

**CLIENT:** Caron/Groupe Revillon, Paris, France

**DESIGNER:** Jean-Pierre Toth, Méthacryl, Paris, France

**DATE OF COMPLETION:** 1990

**PLACE OF SALE:** Caron retail shops

**CLIENT'S BRIEF:** To evoke travel, adventure, discovery –
reflect the product and press release (poster)

## Shiseido Window Display

**CLIENT:** Shiseido, Paris, France

**DESCRIPTION OF PRODUCT:** Shiseido make-up range

**DESIGNER:** Jean-Pierre Toth, Méthacryl, Suresnes, France

## Timberland Interactive Cubes

**CLIENT:** The Timberland Company, Hampton, NH, USA

**DESCRIPTION OF PRODUCT:** Timberland footwear display showing five component parts of footwear construction

**DESIGNERS:** Ron Tise, Vice President – Retail Kevin McCarthy, Director of Store Design and Presentation, Jarvis Brecker, Project Manager, The Timberland Company

**DATE OF COMPLETION:** January 1992

**TARGET MARKET:** For discerning people who value the outdoors and their time in it.

**PLACE OF SALE:** Timberland Specialty Stores, independent footwear and clothing stores, department stores.

**CLIENT'S BRIEF:** To demonstrate, in an interactive way, the core equities of all Timberland products at the point of purchase

**DESIGN RATIONALE:** Timberland's most important achievement has been to design and develop quality footwear, clothing and accessories that last. Many of these products are developed using specific technologies that Timberland has helped pioneer over the last 35 years. These technologies, called Core Equities, are incorporated in most Timberland footwear, clothing and accessories. They consist of waterproof leather, waterproof breathable fabrics and linings, handmade quality workmanship, durable corrosion-proof hardware and comfortable, 100% waterproof direct-attach footwear soles.

## Sample Suitcase for Golden Beauty Range

**CLIENT:** Helena Rubinstein, Boulogne, France

**DESCRIPTION OF PRODUCT:** Portable showcase for Golden Beauty range

**DESIGNER:** Raison Pure, Paris, France

**DATE OF COMPLETION:** March 1992

**TARGET MARKET:** Selective

**PLACE OF SALE:** Department stores and perfumeries

**CLIENT'S BRIEF:** To create a sample case for the sales people which was both elegant and practical, and conveyed the image of the product.

**DESIGN RATIONALE:** A suitcase in which the warm colours of the product were represented in the rich and elegant material of the case itself.

## Lauren Product Glorifier

**CLIENT:** Cosmair, Inc/Ralph Lauren, New York, USA

**DESCRIPTION OF PRODUCT:** Bird's-eye maple, genuine hand-sewn leather, 22K gold plate valve and catch pan, custom-manufactured strap stays, engraved mirror, articulated drawer action.

**DESIGNER:** Consumer Promotion, Inc, New York, USA

**DATE OF COMPLETION:** March 1988

**TARGET MARKET:** Female

**PLACE OF SALE:** Retail department stores

**CLIENT'S BRIEF:** A campaign was established to enhance the richness of the Ralph Lauren 'Lauren' look. The image of country style and elegance was expressed through the use of wood and leather, giving the entire line a specific feeling and tone. These displays heightened customer awareness of a new look that translates into the natural beauty of the outdoors. It conveys the feelings of down-to-earth, fresh air and country life associated with the Lauren woman.

**DESIGN RATIONALE:** Consumer Promotions produced these displays to accomplish a unique and fine piece of well-crafted wood cabinet and mirror box reminiscent of days gone by when quality pieces were built to last – a key factor in the parameters of the well-established ethics of the Ralph Lauren look. This look readily identifies these displays as a Ralph Lauren design statement.

## Sunglasses Display

**CLIENT:** IDC, Marseille, France

**DESCRIPTION OF PRODUCT:** The base and central part of this display are made of enamelled wood. The background is of aluminium, the central decoration is made out of polystyrene mirror. The holders of the sunglasses are of rubber foam with metallic pins in the inside and tips of enamelled wood. Dimensions are: 70 × 40 × 20cm.

**DESIGNER:** RS Creation, Montreuil, France

**DATE OF COMPLETION:** 1989

**TARGET MARKET:** Purchasers of sunglasses

**PLACE OF SALE:** Opticians and gift shops

**CLIENT'S BRIEF:** To create a counter and window display, permitting the display of 12 pairs of glasses. The style of IDC is voluntarily very fashionable, but in a high price zone: the display was supposed to strengthen this image.

**DESIGN RATIONALE:** This brief was translated into a 'look' that is both actual and 'retro'. The use of materials that are at the same time traditional, luxurious and high-tech reinforces this element.

## Essilor Glasses

**CLIENT:** Essilor, Joinville-le-Pont, France

**DESCRIPTION OF PRODUCT:** A display composed of a base of polyurethane foam representing the graphics of a Zen Japanese garden on which were fixed three vertical moulded and tinted wooden elements. These elements are perforated in order to receive small plexiglas tubes which support the glasses. Dimensions are: 50 × 40 × 35cm.

**DESIGNER:** RS Creation, Montreuil, France

**DATE OF COMPLETION:** April 1990

**TARGET MARKET:** Opticians

**PLACE OF SALE:** Specialized retailers

**CLIENT'S BRIEF:** To create a display for a new style of Essilor glasses, dedicated to city customers. The display was supposed to carry the more or less high-tech image of these targeted consumers.

**DESIGN RATIONALE:** As a symbol of the urban universe, three buildings were chosen for the design, which has a plain and restrained style, but is also tough and sophisticated (hence the use of the tinted and varnished wood).

## Killer Loop Sunglass Display

**CLIENT:** Bausch & Lomb, Rochester, NY, USA

**DESCRIPTION OF PRODUCT:** The 'Killer loop' rope cable and sheet steel product holding display

**DESIGNER:** Arnell-Bickford Associates, New York, USA

**MAKER:** Thomson-Leeds Co. Inc., New York, USA

**DATE OF COMPLETION:** Summer 1990

**TARGET MARKET:** United States

**PLACE OF SALE:** Exclusive sporting goods, optical, speciality and department stores

**CLIENT'S BRIEF:** 'Killer loop', the term surfers use to describe a perfect physical performance on a cresting ocean wave, also captures the spirit of a display programme, for Bausch & Lomb's new high-tech, high-performance 'killer loop' line of sunglasses.

**DESIGN RATIONALE:** The 'killer loop' concept, using rope cable and sheet steel, transmits a sense of kinetic energy and provides a practical, product holding display.

## Traction Production Glasses

**CLIENT:** Victor Gros, Traction Production, Clairvaux les Lacs, France

**DESCRIPTION OF PRODUCT:** Metal display stand

**DESIGNER:** Pat PLV, Puteaux, France

**DATE OF COMPLETION:** End of 1990

**PLACE OF SALE:** Opticians

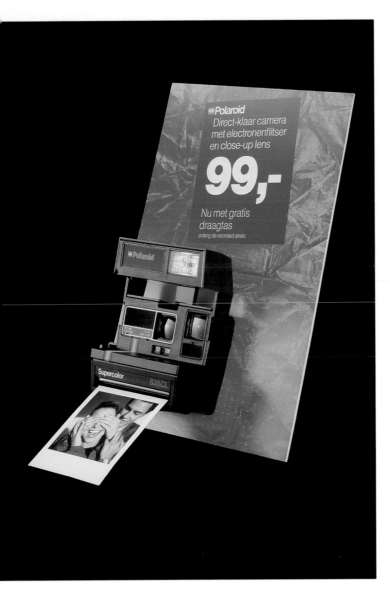

## Polaroid Sunglasses

**CLIENT:** Polaroid Sunglasses, Polaroid Corporation, London, UK

**DESCRIPTION OF PRODUCT:** "Image" Sunglasses packaging and point-of-purchase material

**DESIGNER:** John Rushworth, Theirry Goignat, John Powner, Pentagram Design Ltd, London, UK

**DATE OF COMPLETION:** 1987

**CLIENT'S BRIEF:** The packaging and point-of-purchase material for this exclusive range of Polaroid "Image" sunglasses emphasized the superior quality of the product and highlighted the high specification design. The sunglasses themselves were designed by Pentragram partner Kenneth Grange.

## Polaroid Promotion

**CLIENT:** Polaroid Corporation, London, UK

**DESCRIPTION OF PRODUCT:** Business and professional packaging, point-of-purchase and promotional material

**DESIGNER:** John Rushworth, Bob Mytton, Pentagram Design Ltd, London, UK

**DATE OF COMPLETION:** 1989

**CLIENT'S BRIEF:** Speed, confidentiality and accuracy make Polaroid instant film valuable for business and professional use, and as an effective means of communication. New packaging, point-of-purchase and promotional material was designed to promote this aspect of Polaroid.

## Porto Quinta do Noval

**CLIENT:** Expression F C A, Bordeaux, France

**DESCRIPTION OF PRODUCT:** Lacquered wood, cardboard and vacuum-forming. Dimensions: height 800mm; width 600mm; depth 400mm.

**DESIGNER:** Prisme, Suresnes, France

**DATE OF COMPLETION:** June 1991

**TARGET MARKET:** Port drinkers of any age

**PLACE OF SALE:** Wine stores and high-quality food shops

**CLIENT'S BRIEF:** To create a display counter for 'Quinta do Noval' port that conveys the following messages to the public: Port wine is a product of Portugal; Quinta do Noval is an upper class port. The best way to taste and appreciate port wine is by using a decanter to aerate and let out the aroma.

**DESIGN RATIONALE:** The decanter (an indispensible item for appreciating a good port wine) was made the star of the display by enlarging it to one and a half times its usual size. Each main element is immediately identifiable with Portugal: 'the azulejos' and the richness of their decor and design are seen in a beautiful back drop representing a vineyard. Keeping guard in front of the vines are two bottles of port. One of these is deliberately higher than the other to make it understood that not all 'Quinta do Noval' port wines are the same.

## Class Affair

**CLIENT:** O.D.L.M. Façonnable, Champagne au Mont d'Or, France

**DESCRIPTION OF PRODUCT:** Exotic woods; acrylic mirror; injected-moulded plastic sheet; size: height 430mm; width 590mm; depth 300mm

**DESIGNER:** Prisme, Suresnes, France

**DATE OF COMPLETION:** September 1991

**TARGET MARKET:** Top-end of the range customers, male and female

**PLACE OF SALE:** Opticians

**CLIENT'S BRIEF:** To create a high-quality display for the launch of a new line of tortoiseshell-rimmed regular glasses 'Class Affair'.

**DESIGN RATIONALE:** In Europe the use of wood and Art Deco style are two important trends in interior architecture and decoration, so it was decided to create this environment on a small scale in order to reach the potential consumer. The feeling of fine furniture spotlights the star product in the line. The structure incorporating exotic woods of both light and dark tones underlines the concept of quality. The back mirror gives a feeling of spaciousness.

## Rucanor Shoe Display

**CLIENT:** Rucanor BV, The Netherlands

**DESCRIPTION OF PRODUCT:** Acrylic, lisa, screenprint

**DESIGNER:** Alrec PoS Design, The Netherlands

**DATE OF COMPLETION:** 1991

**TARGET MARKET:** Sports shoe wearers

**PLACE OF SALE:** Sports shoe shops

**CLIENT'S BRIEF:** To design an exclusive shoe display for the introduction of new Rucanor sport shoes.

## Sony Headphones

**CLIENT:** Sony UK Ltd, London, UK

**DESIGNER:** Alrec POS Design, Hillegorn, The Netherlands

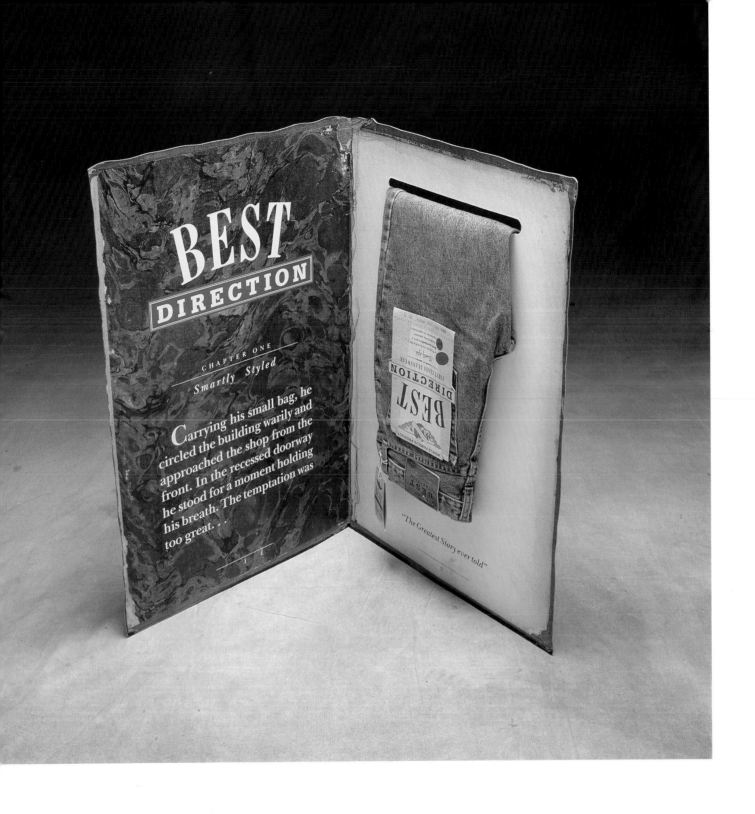

## Best Direction

**CLIENT:** Best Direction Ltd., Greenford, Middlesex, UK

**DESCRIPTION OF PRODUCT:** Free-standing board with slot to hang one pair of jeans

**DESIGNER:** Big Active Ltd, London, UK

**DATE OF COMPLETION:** 1990

**TARGET MARKET:** Male, aged 20–40

**PLACE OF SALE:** High street fashion retail stores

**CLIENT'S BRIEF:** To design an item of point-of-purchase which would display a pair of Best Direction jeans, with a simple construction that was also easy to use.

**DESIGN RATIONALE:** The point-of-purchase item was developed on a theme for Best Direction entitled 'The Greatest Story Ever Told'. The old book design evoked a mood of classic nostalgia. The simple construction enabled the product to be very visible.

## Puiforcat 'Normandy'

**CLIENT:** Puiforcat, La Plaine Saint Denis, France

**DESCRIPTION OF PRODUCT:** Lacquered wood; acrylic sheet; polyurethane foam; size: width 370mm; height 400mm; depth 380mm

**DESIGNER:** Prisme, Suresnes, France

**DATE OF COMPLETION:** November 1990

**TARGET MARKET:** Upper end of the range customers

**PLACE OF SALE:** Department stores and European speciality shops

**CLIENT'S BRIEF:** This place setting was specially designed for the steamship 'Normandy' in 1934. In 1991 it has been re-created for general sales. Puiforcat wanted a small display to emphasize the history of the design and to present the line.

**DESIGN RATIONALE:** To symbolize the steamship 'Normandy' in the clearest fashion, to show the elements of the design. The deck of the ship had to give the perfect presentation for the place setting. It had to be reminiscent of the real ship; the name is spotlighted on the 'bow' of the display. The two acrylic plates symbolize sea foam and waves breaking over the ship and show off the well-known logo 'Puiforcat'.

### Little Cobbler

**CLIENT:** Bally, Paris, France

**DESCRIPTION OF PRODUCT:** Miniature display of cobbler

**DESIGNER:** Bally, Paris, France

**PLACE OF SALE:** Bally retail outlets

## Trifari Tune-In Interactive Marketing Programme

**CLIENT:** Trifari, Inc., New York, NY, USA

**DESCRIPTION OF PRODUCT:** Trifari Tune-In Interactive Marketing Programme

**DESIGNER:** Trans World Marketing, East Rutherford, NJ, USA

**DATE OF COMPLETION:** June 1990

**TARGET MARKET:** Females

**PLACE OF SALE:** Department stores

**CLIENT'S BRIEF:** To educate Trifari consumers on the fundamental basics of accessorizing. To offer the opportunity to generate in-store excitement and multiple purchase of Trifari jewelry through special event promotion.

**DESIGN RATIONALE:** To launch the programme, three jewelry programmes were created: Face Shape, Neckline and Wardrobe Building Analysis. A full-colour Tune-In reference manual visually reinforces the interactive programme, enhances media advertising efforts and assists consumers in selecting from Trifari's 3,000+ jewelry styles.

## Boddington's Keg Bitter and Mild

**CLIENT:** Boddingtons Breweries Limited, Manchester, UK

**DESCRIPTION OF PRODUCT:** Countermounts in metal and bevelled glass

**DESIGNER:** Stephen Gibbons & Malcolm Swatridge, The Partners, London, UK

**DATE OF COMPLETION:** 1989

**TARGET MARKET:** Club and pub customers

**PLACE OF SALE:** Clubs, pubs, etc

**CLIENT'S BRIEF:** The countermounts had to be clearly seen both from the front and from an oblique view along the bar.

## Beer Mats

**CLIENT:** Dryborough, Edinburgh, Scotland, UK

**DESIGNERS:** Stephen Gibbons, David Stuart,
The Partners, London, UK

**ILLUSTRATOR OR PHOTOGRAPHER:** Mick Brownfield

**DATE OF COMPLETION:** 1987

**TARGET MARKET:** A broad cross-section of drinkers

**PLACE OF SALE:** Pubs

**CLIENT'S BRIEF:** To promote a new product at point of
purchase.

**DESIGN RATIONALE:** The beer mats were designed to
reflect a broad range of possible consumers, to create
interest and to encourage their collection.

## Tibere Watches

**CLIENT:** Tibere, Paris, France

**DESCRIPTION OF PRODUCT:** Wood and plastic display
stand

**DESIGNER:** Pat PLV, Puteaux, France

**DATE OF COMPLETION:** End of 1991

**PLACE OF SALE:** Jeweller's shops

Mens and Ladies shapes available in both Flip-up and Fixed Bridge Styles in a range of colours. Australian Made

SOLA CLIP-ONS

## Sola Clip-ons

**CLIENT:** Sola Optical Pty Ltd, Adelaide, South Australia

**DESCRIPTION OF PRODUCT:** Structure for sunglasses

**DESIGNER:** John Nowland, Adelaide, South Australia

**DATE OF COMPLETION:** 1984

**TARGET MARKET:** Clients of optometrists and wearers of prescribed spectacles

**PLACE OF SALE:** Optometrists

**CLIENT'S BRIEF:** System to display maximum number of clip-on sunglasses, easily packed and assembled.

**DESIGN RATIONALE:** Simple, robust, visually interesting system to display clip-on sun lenses. To be located on sales counter in optometrists' offices.

## Royal Blue Display

**CLIENT:** Royal Copenhagen, Copenhagen, Denmark

**DESCRIPTION OF PRODUCT:** Full-size three-winged display

**DESIGNER:** Royal Copenhagen, Denmark

**DATE OF COMPLETION:** Spring 1992

**TARGET MARKET:** Sweden, Italy, USA, UK, Japan and Germany

**PLACE OF SALE:** Porcelain retailers

**CLIENT'S BRIEF:** The three-winged display is part of a comprehensive range of point-of-purchase material developed to support the international Royal Blue campaign from Royal Copenhagen Ltd in-store. The material is meant to supplement the unique beauty, craftsmanship and fine old traditions that lie behind the blue services from Royal Copenhagen.

**DESIGN RATIONALE:** The display enables the shop, with a relatively limited amount of space, to show the full context in which the products are best displayed. Combining the services with cutlery and glassware also produced by Royal Copenhagen in both a classical and a modern version for the younger generation stresses the versatile nature of the blue services.

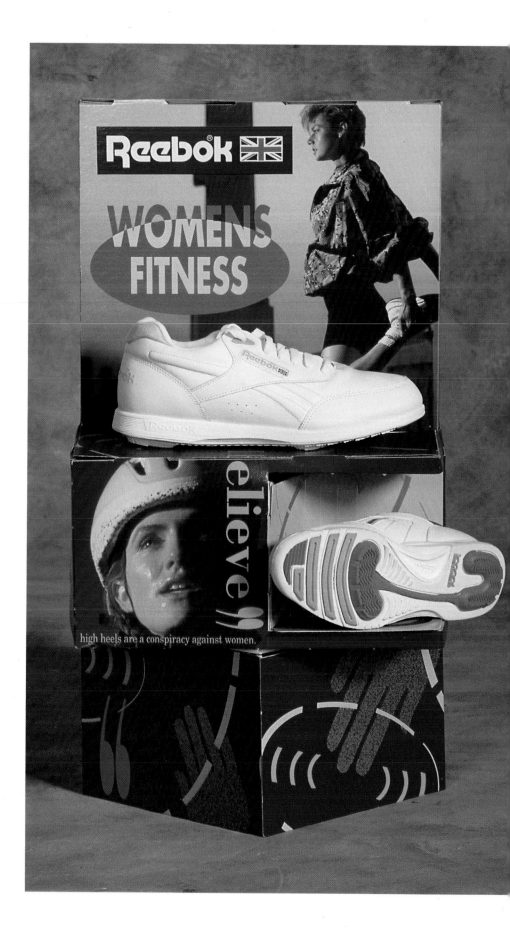

## I Believe

**CLIENT:** Lady Footlocker, New York, USA, and Reebok, Stoughton, Massachusetts, USA

**DESCRIPTION OF PRODUCT:** 18pt board (approx 30 × 72cm)

**DESIGNER:** J P Terlizzi & Susan Bettancourt, Medallion Associates, New York, USA

**DATE OF COMPLETION:** April/May 1992

**TARGET MARKET:** Females aged 19–34

**PLACE OF SALE:** Lady Footlocker (athletic footwear and apparel retailer exclusively for women)

**CLIENT'S BRIEF:** To design a point-of-sale unit that would be utilized on an existing store fixture. The display had to tie into existing Reebok TV and print campaigns and to appeal to women.

**DESIGN RATIONALE:** The aim was to draw the customer into the store so a unit was designed that would be visually exciting. We didn't want to see the existing unit so we developed the stacked boxes. We wanted to emphasize that it was for women so we utilized mezzotints of each woman and enlarged them utilizing each women's 'Belief in fitness'. The shoes were displayed on top of the boxes so that the customer would need to walk all around the display. The colours were designed to complement store colours.

## "L'Art de Vivre"

**CLIENT:** Flammarion 4, Paris, France

**DESCRIPTION OF PRODUCT:** Display unit; size 540 × 340 × 200mm to sell boxed sets of postcards and envelopes

**DESIGNER:** Flammarion 4, Paris, France

**DATE OF COMPLETION:** 1992

**PLACE OF SALE:** Booksellers

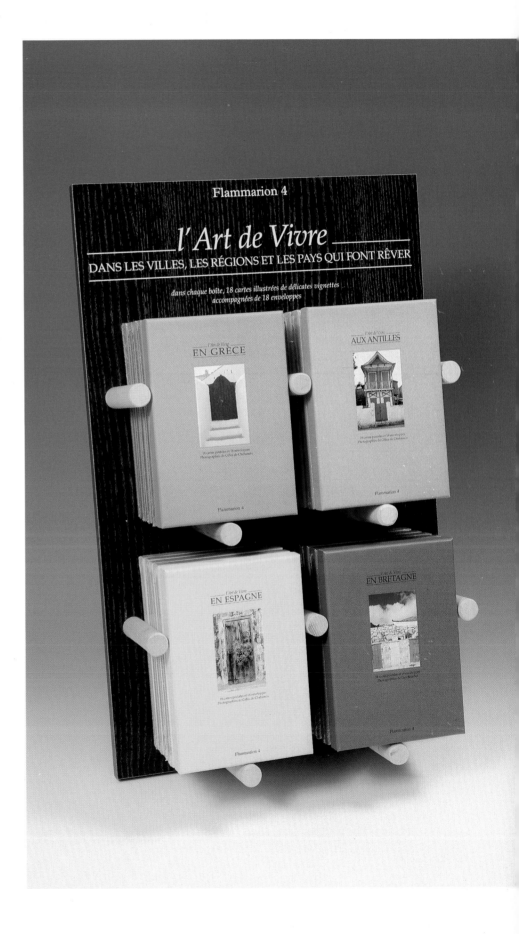

**Product dispensers** The structures in this chapter not only present and promote products, they are also specifically designed to allow us access. They contain quantities of a product and products rather than one perfectly presented specimen, and they keep them neatly arranged, are easy to examine, and most important of all, are easy to replenish. They extend the image of the product or the identity of the manufacturer. In some cases they indicate the price and the sales message, and they don't fall over!

But these are only the fundamentals of the brief. The designs also present their products in an isolated little environment that adds impact, prestige and clarity in the often chaotic surroundings of the shop floor.

## London Life

**CLIENT:** London Life, Bristol, UK

**DESCRIPTION OF PRODUCT:** Dispenser made from solid oak

**DESIGNER:** Aziz Cami & Stephen Gibbons, The Partners, London, UK

**MAKER:** Toby Winteringham

**ILLUSTRATOR OR PHOTOGRAPHER:** Brian McIntyre

**DATE OF COMPLETION:** 1988

**TARGET MARKET:** Wealthy consumer/financial product purchasers

**PLACE OF SALE:** Headquarters and regional offices of London Life

**CLIENT'S BRIEF:** Publication design is built around the way London Life does business, putting together a financial package for each individual client. All items of literature have to co-ordinate, since any combination could be appropriate. The Partners used the core idea of the nest egg, and devised witty variations to suit a Supersave Plan, a VIP Pension Scheme, or whatever.

**DESIGN RATIONALE:** The overall nest egg idea means that any combinations of product brochures can be assembled into a unified package for an individual client.

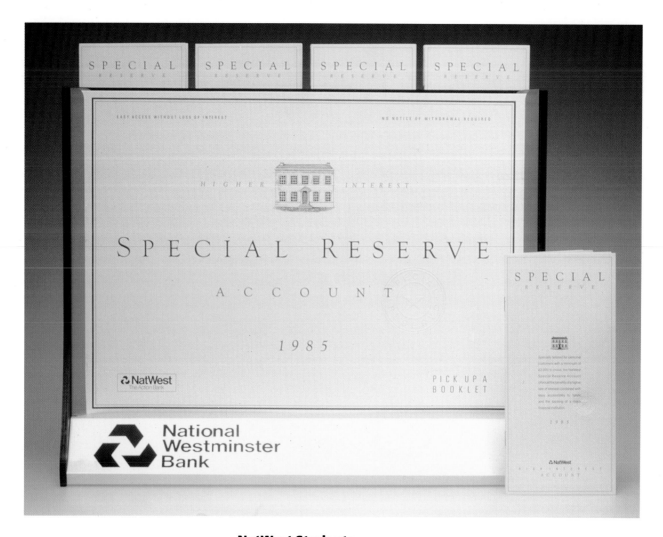

### NatWest Students

**CLIENT:** NatWest Bank, London, UK

**DESCRIPTION OF PRODUCT:** Student leaflet and posters

**DESIGNER:** Michael Johnson, Smith & Milton, London, UK

**PHOTOGRAPHERS:** Martin Barrand, Trevor Key, Frank Farrelly, Inga Middleton

**TARGET MARKET:** 18+ new students on campus

**PLACE OF SALE:** In branches of NatWest and at Freshers' Fairs

## Natwest Gold Plus

**CLIENT:** National Westminster Bank, London, UK

**DESCRIPTION OF PRODUCT:** Counter-top dispenser and brochure

**DESIGNER:** Minale Tattersfield & Partners Ltd, Richmond, Surrey, UK

**DATE OF COMPLETION:** 1986

**TARGET MARKET:** Gold Plus is NatWest's Premier financial service

**PLACE OF SALE:** Distributed from NatWest branches

**CLIENT'S BRIEF:** The brief from NatWest was to create a high-quality product with a select identity for this up-market target audience, in order to convey the considerable benefits package on offer from the NatWest Gold Plus service.

**DESIGN RATIONALE:** The design of the 'Gold Bar' which held the brochure reflected the value of the service.

## Sara Midda Promotion

**CLIENT:** Pan Books, London, UK

**DESCRIPTION OF PRODUCT:** Posters and dump bins for
*Sketchbook from Southern France*

**DATE OF COMPLETION:** 1991

**PLACE OF SALE:** Bookshops

## Michael Jackson;
## *The Legend Continues*
## (video)

**CLIENT:** Vestron Musicvideo, Stamford, Connecticut, USA

**DESCRIPTION OF PRODUCT:** Michael Jackson point-of-purchase display and video-tape packaging. Corrugated cardboard: 4ft high × 1ft wide

**DESIGNER:** Tim Nihoff and Scott Nash, Corey McPherson Nash, Watertown, MA, USA

**ILLUSTRATOR OR PHOTOGRAPHER:** Various

**DATE OF COMPLETION:** 1989

**TARGET MARKET:** Michael Jackson fans, young music lovers

**PLACE OF SALE:** Record stores and discount department stores

**CLIENT'S BRIEF:** To design the video-tape packaging and point-of-purchase display.

**DESIGN RATIONALE:** The display is designed to work both as a table-top and free-standing display. The portion of the display that holds the tapes is designed so that when the stock of tapes are used or removed, the image of the packaging remains.

## Trifari Department Store Jewelry Fixture

**CLIENT:** Trifari, Inc, New York, NY, USA

**DESCRIPTION OF PRODUCT:** Trifari Department Store Jewelry Fixture Programme

**DESIGNER:** Trans World Marketing, East Rutherford, NJ, USA

**DATE OF COMPLETION:** May 1990

**TARGET MARKET:** Females

**PLACE OF SALE:** Department stores

**CLIENT'S BRIEF:** To develop a unified department store refixturing programme, encompassing all aspects of Trifari's quality fashion jewelry line. To convey a sleek, contemporary image, yet offer superior functionality and space-efficient product presentation. To provide security, while affording easy customer access and shopability.

**DESIGN RATIONALE:** A contemporary colour scheme and dominant brand identification unify the entire programme, producing an elegant department store image. The displays illustrate innovative merchandizing, through use of a revolutionary wanding capability, as well as easy-to-operate pilfer-resistant merchanisms. The airy design of the displays enables Trifari sales personnel to have clear visibility of the entire jewelry counter area. Specially matched paper was used to create the marbelized look on tower headers and earring cards. The marbelized label on the surface of each tower hides slots which can be used for future earring bar placement.

## Sarah Coventry Interactive Merchandizing Programme

**CLIENT:** R. N. Koch, Inc., Sarah Coventry Jewelry, Pawtucket, Rhode Island, USA

**DESCRIPTION OF PRODUCT:** Sarah Coventry Interactive Merchandizing Programme

**DESIGNER:** Trans World Marketing, East Rutherford, NJ, USA

**DATE OF COMPLETION:** February 1989

**TARGET MARKET:** Females

**PLACE OF SALE:** Mass merchandizers

**CLIENT'S BRIEF:** To revitalize the Sarah Coventry brand name and establish a high-quality image for a redesigned line of costume jewelry for the mass market.

**DESIGN RATIONALE:** To create a contemporary, eye-catching overall appearance that conveyed the department store image of Sarah Coventry Jewelry; and to provide space-efficient product merchandizing by use of rotating towers and individual earring panels in a relatively small footprint.

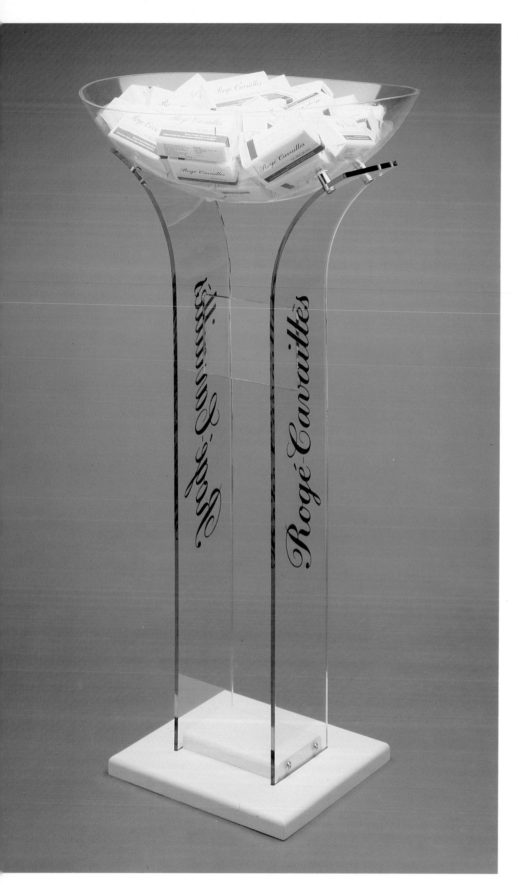

## Rogé Cavailles

**CLIENT:** Procter and Gamble, Neuilly Sur Seine, France

**DESCRIPTION OF PRODUCT:** Lacquered wood; acrylic vacuum-forming; curved acrylic; size: height 1070mm; diameter 500mm

**DESIGNER:** Prisme, Suresnes, France

**DATE OF COMPLETION:** September 1991

**TARGET MARKET:** Everybody

**PLACE OF SALE:** Pharmacies and drugstores

**CLIENT'S BRIEF:** Since its creation in 1932, Rogé Cavailles soap has been recommended by both druggists and dermatologists. Although the products will be presented in a basket, the objective is to create a floor display with a special design to emphasize the quality, the purity and the legitimacy of Rogé Cavailles soaps.

**DESIGN RATIONALE:** The inspiration was 'Art Deco' style directly related to the creation of the product in 1932. The pure shape is in the form of a special and unique object. The high-quality materials reinforce this feeling. The display is designed to recall the bathroom and its environment: the use of transparent material evokes water, the use of a basin is to simulate the washbasin, so that the product is directly related to its function.

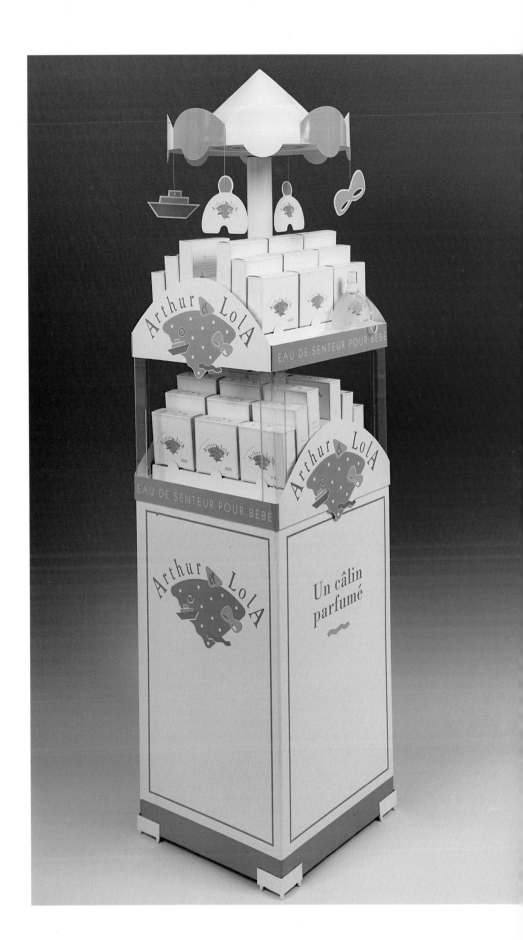

## Arthur et Lola

**CLIENT:** Pharmhygiène, le Plessis Robinson, France

**DESCRIPTION OF PRODUCT:** Arthur et Lola floor-stand display

**DESIGNER:** Ateliers Reunis, Bagnolet, France

**DATE OF COMPLETION:** Winter 1991/92

**PLACE OF SALE:** Drugstores/pharmacies

**CLIENT'S BRIEF:** To create a floor-stand display for short-life direction for a new market area – baby perfume. The display needed to be accessible, light and compact.

**DESIGN RATIONALE:** The unit at the top of the display turns to attract attention; the display unit was cheap to produce and easy to move and clean, and it aroused the customer's curiosity – the aim of the point-of-purchase material for this new product.

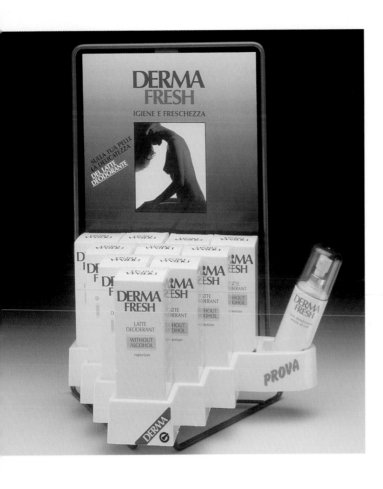

## Derma

**CLIENT:** Biochimici P.S.N., Bologna, Italy

**DESCRIPTION OF PRODUCT:** Structure for products, sizes
– small: 42 × 29 × 23cm; large: 190 × 50 × 45cm

**DESIGNER:** Studio Bonomi, Italy

**ILLUSTRATOR OR PHOTOGRAPHER:** Studio Bonomi

**DATE OF COMPLETION:** 1990–91

**TARGET MARKET:** High level

**PLACE OF SALE:** Pharmacies

**CLIENT'S BRIEF:** To create a floor-standing and counter-
top display structure for a vast range of products. To
create synthesized leaflet information for the customers.

**DESIGN RATIONALE:** To underline in both colours and
materials the varied lines of different Derma products,
and to make a suitable space for a product tester in the
structure.

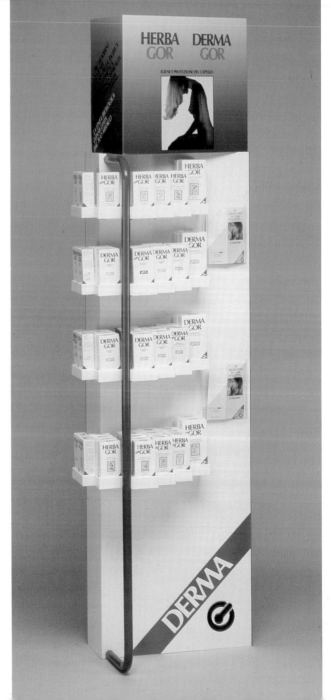

## Studio Line Ravviva Ricci

**CLIENT:** Saipo L'Oreal, Torino, Italy

**DESCRIPTION OF PRODUCT:** Polystyrene carton: size 38 × 32 × 22in

**DESIGNER:** Studio Bonomi, Italy

**ILLUSTRATOR OR PHOTOGRAPHER:** Agenzia Pubblicitaria Della Oreal

**DATE OF COMPLETION:** 1990–1991

**TARGET MARKET:** Upper end youth market

**PLACE OF SALE:** Perfumeries

**CLIENT'S BRIEF:** To create a counter-top display which is both economical in terms of scale and takes the largest possible number of products; to unite the information leaflets in a single style.

## Coca-Cola Jukebox Cooler

**CLIENT:** Coca Cola Co Ltd, New York, USA

**DESCRIPTION OF PRODUCT:** Constructed of glossy high-impact plastic with leak-proof drainage system with spigot

**DESIGNER:** Paul Flum Ideas Inc, New York, USA

**DATE OF COMPLETION:** Ongoing promotions

**TARGET MARKET:** To attract consumers to mass displays in supermarkets, hypermarkets etc.

**PLACE OF SALE:** Supermarkets, hypermarkets etc. (point-of-sale in retail chains)

**DESIGN RATIONALE:** The design is guaranteed to attract attention. It is a replica of a 1950s jukebox, featuring an insulated ice bin, glossy high-impact plastic construction and beautiful details. It is ideal as a dynamic dealer's leader, a great consumer premium, and as a perfect sampling unit.

## Coca-Cola Nostalgia Cooler II

**CLIENT:** Coca Cola Co Ltd, New York, USA

**DESCRIPTION OF PRODUCT:** This cooler is a replica of a 1950's vending machine. It is constructed of glossy, high-impact plastic, detailed with authentic graphics and features a guaranteed drain system with spigot. Holds 99 12oz cans; 52 16oz bottles; 40 20oz bottles

**DESIGNER:** Paul Flum Ideas Inc, New York, USA

**DATE OF COMPLETION:** Ongoing promotions

**TARGET MARKET:** Consumers at supermarkets, hypermarkets

**PLACE OF SALE:** Supermarkets, hypermarkets (point-of-sale in retail chains)

**DESIGN RATIONALE:** The Nostalgia Cooler II was designed to guarantee placements in the highest quality, best traffic locations. It is also ideal as a dealer-loader and as a great consumer premium.

## Seven-Up Giant Bottle

**DESCRIPTION OF PRODUCT:** Ice cabinet for 116 12oz cans; 72 16oz bottles; 58 20oz bottles

**DESIGNER:** Paul Flum Ideas Inc, New York, USA

**DATE OF COMPLETION:** Ongoing promotions

**TARGET MARKET:** Consumers in convenience stores, supermarkets, fast food outlets, gas mini-marts etc.

**PLACE OF SALE:** For point-of-sale displays in retail outlets

**DESIGN RATIONALE:** The giant bottle iceman is designed to replicate a Seven-Up bottle to attract consumers for increased single-serve sales. The unique bottle top end features openings in which consumers can reach through to obtain the products without taking off the lid.

## Ultrabrite

**CLIENT:** Colgate Palmolive, Courbevoie, France

**DESCRIPTION OF PRODUCT:** Gondola or island display in double wall corrugated board printed in two colours flexo. Hand-mounted in 4 minutes. Transports in pallet size case, 800 × 600 × 150mm

**DESIGNER:** Stream-line, Paris, France

**DATE OF COMPLETION:** September 1990

**TARGET MARKET:** General public

**PLACE OF SALE:** Hypermarkets

**CLIENT'S BRIEF:** For Ultrabrites' fresh and vibrant image – a line extension around toothpaste into personal cosmetics – roll on, spray, shower gel, eau de toilette. All products to be displayed at the same time in a single easy-to-construct display. Ultrabrite has a strong, monolithic, clean, fresh image, to be reflected in an impressive, imposing design. Must hold over 250kg (¼ tonne).

**DESIGN RATIONALE:** The style – imposing, impressive, tall and dark – reflects Ultrabrite's brand identity. Vertical graphics on corner supports enhance the effect. Solid and inventive board engineering creates a stable structure that is easy to put up *in situ* and easy to fill and display. One pallet holds all products and the display mounting in the flat.

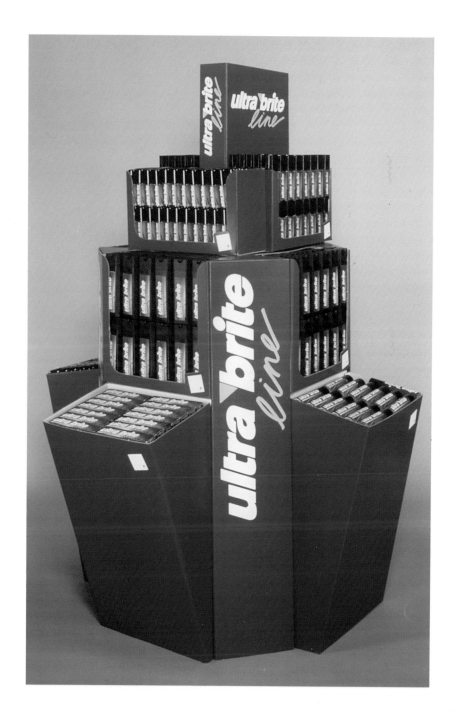

## L.A. Looks Cosmetic Kit

**CLIENT:** Los Angeles Research Packaging, Los Angeles, California, USA

**DESCRIPTION OF PRODUCT:** Make-up kits containing eye shadows and blushers. One dozen kits in a point-of-purchase display.

**DESIGNER:** Mamoru Shimokochi, Anne Reeves, Tracy McGoldrick, Shimokochi/Reeves Design, Los Angeles, California, USA

**DATE OF COMPLETION:** Christmas 1991

**TARGET MARKET:** 13–15 age group

**PLACE OF SALE:** Mass merchandise and drug stores in the USA

**CLIENT'S BRIEF:** Due to the success of the LA Looks hair styling line, it was decided to extend the brand image to a Cosmetic Kit targeted at the young teens. The Cosmetic Kit package and point-of-purchase had to reflect the same fun, Southern California attitude and project the quality and feeling of the LA Looks styling line – appealing to those who aspire to the youthful LA image. The purchase was seasonal, planned for the Christmas and back-to-school market.

**DESIGN RATIONALE:** The Cosmetic kit and point-of-purchase captures the fun and excitement of the original LA Looks styling line. A unique identity was created for the Cosmetic Kit through the use of vibrant colour and graphic elements, projecting a gift-like quality.

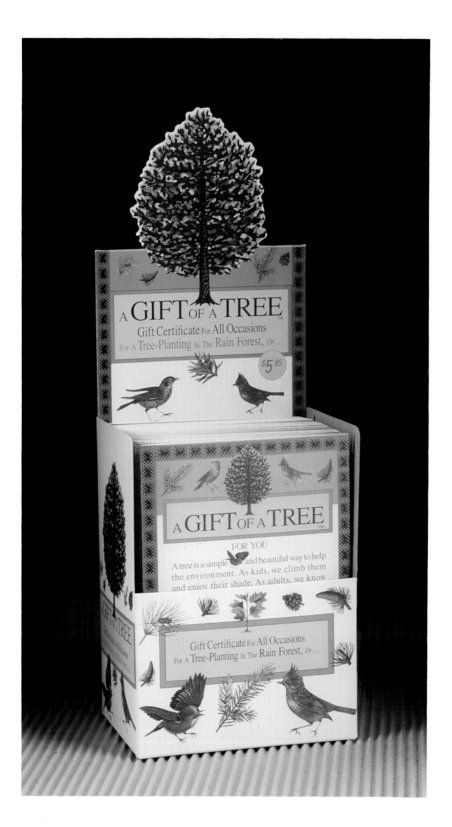

## A Gift of a Tree

**CLIENT:** Earth Plan, Sherman Oaks, California, USA

**DESCRIPTION OF PRODUCT:** A gift certificate greeting card for a tree-planting kit and display box, printed on recycled paper

**DESIGNER:** Mamoru Shimokochi, Anne Reeves, Shimokochi/Reeves Design, Los Angeles, California, USA

**DATE OF COMPLETION:** 1991

**TARGET MARKET:** Environmentally conscious consumers and the general public

**PLACE OF SALE:** Throughout the USA

**CLIENT'S BRIEF:** A new and unique product concept. A gift certificate greetings card which helps the environment. Each certificate represents the planting of a tree. The objective: to develop a strong point-of-purchase item to display the earth-sensitive greetings cards and reflect trees and the environment.

**DESIGN RATIONALE:** The design reflects the uniqueness of the gift certificate concept and the concern for the environment. The use of recycled paper, and fine detailed line drawings of trees and birds, further strengthen the overall message and sensitivity to the cause.

## Sarah Coventry Small Leather Goods

**CLIENT:** RGA, New York, NY, USA

**DESCRIPTION OF PRODUCT:** Women's leather purses, wallets; 2 sizes only

**DESIGNER:** Barry Berger, Art Martin, Tom Stoeckle, Heidi Sklenar, Barry David Berger + Associates, Inc., New York, NY, USA

**ILLUSTRATOR OR PHOTOGRAPHER:** Julian Kaiser

**DATE OF COMPLETION:** 1990

**TARGET MARKET:** Mass merchandizers

**PLACE OF SALE:** K-Mart, Walmart, Sears

**CLIENT'S BRIEF:** To develop a 100% recyclable gift package that displays its contents (women's wallets, cheque books) so that all of the product's details are seen/touched easily; to develop a display that holds two each of 60 styles and induces the retailer to use the display.

**DESIGN RATIONALE:** The gift package provides full product access. Two sizes are available. The display fixture's tray is open to eliminate trash and angles downward so that it "housekeeps" itself by using centrifugal force to guarantee that all packages are positioned forward. The retailer is more likely to use the display, which increases the rate of sales.

## Displays Cachou Lajaunie

**CLIENT:** Cachou Lajaunie, Toulouse, France

**DESCRIPTION OF PRODUCT:** Both the displays are made out of a backing of formed and injected polystyrene (to obtain a very low fabrication cost)

**DESIGNER:** RS Creation, Montreuil, France

**DATE OF COMPLETION:** Display 1 1986; Display 2 1989

**TARGET MARKET:** Any

**PLACE OF SALE:** Tobacco shops, service stations, drugstores.

**CLIENT'S BRIEF:** The goal was to create a stocking display that was as small as possible, manufactured in very large numbers (40,000 samples), valourizing the product and carrying an image which was both 'going back to the past' and 'in fashion' for this revived product.

**DESIGN RATIONALE:** Through its design the first project is reminiscent of the very old radios, the Wurlitzer juke boxes and the old French milestone. In the header card, the facing of an oversized tin was integrated. The design is voluntarily 'back to the past'.

The second project is a renewal of the first but with two new factors: an optimal visualization of the product and the integration of a new flavour of the product, which explains the double signature.

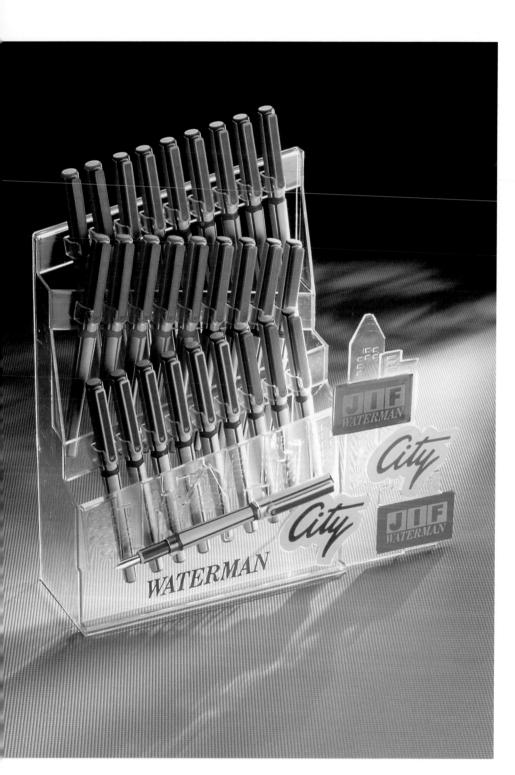

## City

**CLIENT:** Waterman SA, Paris, France

**DESCRIPTION OF PRODUCT:** One piece injection-moulded display with engraving and silkscreen print. Mould is a simple two-piece without sliders.

**DESIGNER:** Stream-line, Paris, France

**DATE OF COMPLETION:** September 1989

**TARGET MARKET:** Students and schoolchildren

**PLACE OF SALE:** All stationers, bookshops, kiosks etc.

**CLIENT'S BRIEF:** For a new range of pens aimed at schoolchildren and students, Waterman were looking for a counter display that set off the products on a fashionable background. The display had to be economic, low in tooling costs, filled in the factory and immediately usable by retailers.

**DESIGN RATIONALE:** Stream-line invented a 'Big City' theme, with a flashing neon and skyscraper background, to set off this fashionable and colourful pen. The pens are suspended by an innovative moulding detail, and soar in crossed banks into the air. The front panel carries the big city in relief.

## Timex Watches

**CLIENT:** Timex, Waterbury, Connecticut, USA

**DESCRIPTION OF PRODUCT:** Showcase

**DESIGNER:** Barry David Berger & Associates Inc, New York, USA

**CLIENT'S BRIEF:** It was the first package to re-design in nine years. It had to be among first gift packages under Christmas tree to be opened; it had to have high-tech package styling to overcome a stodgy product image.

**DESIGN RATIONALE:** The main elements of the design rationale were: it had to be easy to gift wrap; it had to have minimum left-to-right dimension; it had to have maximum internal volume. The display graphics had to be keyed to the consumer's lifestyle and to the product's design. The point-of-purchase fixture had to appear like a museum showcase and to light every product evenly and equally.

## Visolaire

**CLIENT:** Dr van der Hoog, Netherlands

**DESCRIPTION OF PRODUCT:** Skin-care cosmetics

**DESIGNER:** Stadium Design BV, Hillegom, Netherlands

**DATE OF COMPLETION:** Spring 1991

**TARGET MARKET:** Upper level purchasers of cosmetics

## Tops

**CLIENT:** Bryant & May Ltd, High Wycombe, Bucks, UK

**DESCRIPTION OF PRODUCT:** Matches

**DESIGNER:** Michael Sheridan & Co Ltd, 40 Nelson St, Leicester, UK

**DATE OF COMPLETION:** 1989

**TARGET MARKET:** Smokers, middle market, 16–45 years

**PLACE OF SALE:** Confectioners, tobacconists and newsagents

**CLIENT'S BRIEF:** To display the product and get the maximum stock-holding in retail outlets where space is at a premium. A permanent merchanizer for use in CTNs and pubs. The matches are positioned as a fashion accessory for smokers and command a premium price.

**DESIGN RATIONALE:** High-volume manufacture and quality of presentation resulted in an injection-moulded gravity-feed merchandizer/dispenser with good product visibility. Vertical stock-holding ensures high-stockholding-to-space occupancy. Base is removable for wall positioning as well as standard counter or shelf positioning.

## Letraset

**CLIENT:** Letraset, Paramus, New Jersey, USA

**DESCRIPTION OF PRODUCT:** Professional zylon-base markers

**DESIGNER:** Barry David Berger & Associates, Inc, New York, USA

**ILLUSTRATOR OR PHOTOGRAPHER:** Barry David Berger & Associates, Inc

**PLACE OF SALE:** Art materials retailers, design professionals

**CLIENT'S BRIEF:** To increase the client's market share by: providing the most effective point-of-purchase fixtures to retailers whose clients purchase markers through visits to retail art material stores; providing the most flexible, effective marker organizer for retailers to give or sell to clients who purchase markers by phone or fax orders. To provide both the desk-top organizer and the modular point-of-purchase fixture by using as many identical parts as possible, to reduce capital investment.

**DESIGN RATIONALE:** Letraset's markers' colours are keyed to the Pantone colour matching system. Their labels are carefully printed to match their ink colours. The left/right priority marker cassette permits extreme close-packing while allowing the shopper to 'open' the display fixture at any location, and the front/back hinge allows easy access to pre-selected palettes.

## Oh My Goodness (instant oriental noodle packaging)

**CLIENT:** Myojo Foods of America, Inc, New York, USA

**DESCRIPTION OF PRODUCT:** Japanese eggless ramen in six flavours

**DESIGNER:** Robert P. Gersin Assoc. Inc, New York, USA

**DATE OF COMPLETION:** 1979

**TARGET MARKET:** American consumers through grocery stores, supermarkets and convenience stores

**PLACE OF SALE:** As above

**CLIENT'S BRIEF:** To develop appropriate positioning and package to introduce a ramen product manufactured in Japan to the American market . It had to appeal to consumers who view a noodle dish as an accompaniment to a main dish or as a snack. It also had to create a distinctive system of packages that would compete on the grocers' shelf with a variety of other similar products and allow for line extension.

**DESIGN RATIONALE:** The soft packs are difficult for the retailer to display neatly. The shipper display carton allowed the grocer to get at die-cut sections for pricing (without removing them) and neatly displayed the product. The packages remain fresh-looking for the consumer.

## Toblerone

**CLIENT:** Suchard Ltd, Cheltenham, Glos., UK

**DESCRIPTION OF PRODUCT:** Counter display unit for Toblerone 35g bars. Vac-formed, coloured PVC and acetate print, 12in high

**DESIGNER:** J Schwartz, Cheltenham, Glos., UK

**ILLUSTRATOR OR PHOTOGRAPHER:** Link Marketing Design

**DATE OF COMPLETION:** January 1992

**TARGET MARKET:** Male and female consumers of Toblerone, 20–35 years old

**PLACE OF SALE:** Specifically designed to increase display within the newsagent, tobacconist and confectioners' stores

**CLIENT'S BRIEF:** To design a 'disposable' display unit for Toblerone that would secure space for the brand near the prime cash register area. The unit would probably be discarded after two months by the retailer and therefore the increased sales generated by the display would have to cover the units costs within this period.

**DESIGN RATIONALE:** Space is very precious for the retailer and therefore the unit would only be used if it took up as little surface area as possible. By putting the stock 'up in the air' a box of bars can be stored using only a fraction of the surface area. The bars create the display's branding.

## Systema Hair Care

**CLIENT:** Sebastian, Woodland Hills, California, USA

**DESCRIPTION OF PRODUCT:** Systema point-of-purchase display. Injection-moulded to display the Systema Hair Care Line. The display measures 18in × 17in × 17in approximately.

**DESIGNER:** Stuart Karten Design, Marina del Rey, California, USA

**ILLUSTRATOR OR PHOTOGRAPHER:** Domenic Marsden

**DATE OF COMPLETION:** 1988

**TARGET MARKET:** Females aged 15–30

**PLACE OF SALE:** Professional hair salons

**CLIENT'S BRIEF:** To create an interesting, eye-catching counter display to support two to three examples of each product.

**DESIGN RATIONALE:** Systema, The Elements of Design, was the client's name for the product line. The tag line 'Elements of Design' was capitalized on by constructing the display from the three-dimensional elements of design: the cone and cube and sphere. These elements were floated on an organic form and bridged with shelves to support the product. The dynamics of all these elements created a striking overall form that attracted the customer to the display.

**Coordinated schemes** Design companies and marketing
departments, once they have designed a new product, will look for ways of
extending the imagery to broaden its exposure and increase its impact. In a
bank or a building society, leaflets and showcards, dispensers, posters and
window graphics can all be designed to coordinate. The image of a new or
redesigned product can be extended to include dumpbins and signage. A new
musical or pop event will have a continuity of graphics – from the posters and
advertising to the programmes and the T-shirts of its ushers and backstage
crew.

## Camper Brutus

**CLIENT:** Camper-Coflusa, Mallorca, Spain

**DESCRIPTION OF PRODUCT:** Display for a shoe style

**DESIGNER:** Carlos Rolando, CR Communication & Design Services, Barcelona, Spain

**DATE OF COMPLETION:** 1988

**TARGET MARKET:** People of any age

**PLACE OF SALE:** Camper shops all over Spain

**CLIENT'S BRIEF:** Camper communication philosophy

consists in never showing the shoes in photographs, but using an eclectic, sometimes naïve, sometimes intellectual approach, through illustration or methaphor, thus creating a peculiar communication style built on many different graphic forms.

**DESIGN RATIONALE:** In the case of this product, the creative concept was based on creating a brand identity for this kind of working shoes. By using strong graphics, the product is given a more trendy image.

# B R U T U S

## Airmiles

**CLIENT:** Natwest Bank, London, UK

**DESCRIPTION OF PRODUCT:** Point-of-sale posters and leaflets

**DESIGNER:** Michael Johnson, Smith & Milton, London, UK

**ILLUSTRATOR:** Michael Johnson, Janice Davison

**TARGET MARKET:** Natwest Airmiles collectors/potential collectors

**PLACE OF SALE:** In branches

**CLIENT'S BRIEF:** To encourage subscriptions to airmiles schemes by *saving* money, rather than spending. For every £10 saved, subscribers received one airmile.

**DESIGN RATIONALE:** "Save with us, fly free" was a working copyline that became real when we took a mile of air and showed it in the plane shape. We could then take the symbol and change it and play a few humorous games to help people see where they could fly to.

## Dillons

**CLIENT:** Pearce Retailing Ltd, Birmingham, UK

**DESIGNER:** Stocks Taylor Benson Ltd, Leics, UK

**ILLUSTRATOR OR PHOTOGRAPHER:** Copyright-Free Images

**DATE OF COMPLETION:** February 1990

**TARGET MARKET:** ABC male/female equal bias, 25–60 years

**PLACE OF SALE:** Dillons, Athena Bookstores (approximately 100 outlets)

**CLIENT'S BRIEF:** To create an Easter visual identity appropriate to the religious timing without resorting directly to crucifixion images.

**DESIGN RATIONALE:** The use of architectural style illustrations of churches hit the right balance between religion and seriousness, but was still attractive and sophisticated.

## Natwest Car Loans

**CLIENT:** National Westminster Bank, London, UK

**DESCRIPTION OF PRODUCT:** 2ft × 2ft posters mounted on card for display

**DESIGNER:** Minale, Tattersfield & Partners Limited, Richmond, Surrey, UK

**ILLUSTRATOR OR PHOTOGRAPHER:** Minale Tattersfield

**DATE OF COMPLETION:** 1988

**TARGET MARKET:** Aimed at NatWest customers who may require a loan to buy a car

**PLACE OF SALE:** All NatWest branches

**CLIENT'S BRIEF:** To design a range of large posters that could be displayed within NatWest branches to support the brochures available on NatWest car loans

**DESIGN RATIONALE:** Key points in the NatWest Car Loans Brochure (also designed by MTP) are illustrated by familiar symbols taken from a car's dashboard. These adapt for large posters and panels.

## Second Image Jeanswear

**CLIENT:** Second Image Limited, Greenford, Middlesex, UK

**DESCRIPTION OF PRODUCT:** Enamel wall signs/free standing (×2), jeanswear/denim display, shelf/counter stand

**DESIGNER:** Big-Active Limited, London, UK

**DATE OF COMPLETION:** 1989

**TARGET MARKET:** Basic jeanswear consumers (male & female) aged 15–35

**PLACE OF SALE:** Specialist jeanswear retailers/departments

**CLIENT'S BRIEF:** To develop a point-of-purchase kit suitable for mailing. Flexibility and display of product were important considerations given the variety of in-store environments that the kit would have to work within.

**DESIGN RATIONALE:** The identity of the brand was animated over a series of items to evoke a sense of the display belonging to a bygone age. The story created gives a unique insight into the world projected by second image jeanswear.

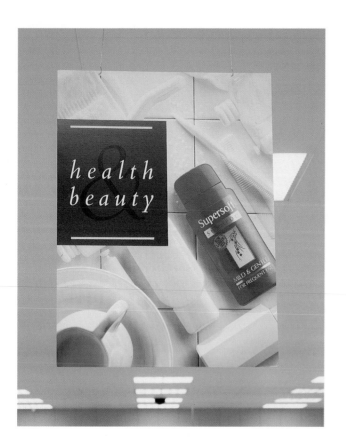

## Health & Beauty

**CLIENT:** Tesco Stores Ltd, Cheshunt, Hertfordshire, UK

**DESCRIPTION OF PRODUCT:** Hanging boards and display stand

**DESIGNER:** Andrew Kibble/Neil Hoye, Jones & Co Design Ltd, London, UK

**ILLUSTRATOR OR PHOTOGRAPHER:** Paul Kemp

**DATE OF COMPLETION:** Summer 1991

**TARGET MARKET:** People who shop at Tesco but normally buy health and beauty products at other pharmacies and chemists

**PLACE OF SALE:** Tesco superstores

**CLIENT'S BRIEF:** Identity and promotion was needed for the Health and Beauty department, encouraging the exploration by the customer of the area. It was also important to stimulate the purchase of a variety of products normally bought elsewhere, and to promote various brands within a scheme that suggested other purchases without detracting from the brand's impact.

**DESIGN RATIONALE:** It was decided to photograph the brands in their relevant situations but to heighten their impact by using only white and clear props. This reinforced the clean and fresh cosmetic appeal and allowed other products to stimulate purchase without detracting from the brand.

## "K"

**CLIENT:** Garner Group, Bristol, UK

**DESIGNER:** Simpson Fitzherbert (SFB), London, UK

**DATE OF COMPLETION:** 1991

## Rowenta Irons

**CLIENT:** Rowenta, Cambridge, Massachusetts, USA

**DESCRIPTION OF PRODUCT:** Iron

**DESIGNER:** Barry David Berger & Associates Inc,
New York, USA

**TARGET MARKET:** High-end consumer

**PLACE OF SALE:** Department stores, speciality stores

**CLIENT'S BRIEF:** Irons are promoted at retail outlets by
live demonstrations. The standard display mode is on-
shelf. Department stores accept no client supplied
displays so the designer must provide a display device
that: appears high-end and compatible with product;
provides detailed copy to differentiate up to six models;
and is removable for live demonstrations; can be
re-attached without hardware and tools; and can be
permanently removed without residue so that display
product is not lost for sale.

**DESIGN RATIONALE:** The injection moulding and hot-
stamped plaque follows the only part of the iron that is
common to all models; attaches with industrial-quality
velcro and removable double-sided tape; allows left-or
right-handed demonstrators to use the iron with or
without the attached plaque; and requires little
additional shelf space.

**In-store systems** The apotheosis of point of purchase is the complete graphic treatment of an entire environment. During the retail boom of the 1980s design companies began to employ not only graphics and interior designers, but product designers, architects, space planners and even market researchers and retail analysts.

The design of a new store could include its name and corporate identity, its stationery, its ticketing and signage, its vans and head office, its shelving, carpets, lighting and interior ambience. And, of course, its point of purchase Graphics to promote product areas, special offers and sale items, were no longer simply hung from the ceiling, but could be incorporated into perimeter shelving, wall treatments and window displays. Price ticketing was designed to fit in with the overall colours and materials, graphic panels were held in place by specially designed fixtures that were not brought from shopfitters standard ranges. The result was a coordinated environment which supported the client's products and philosophy, and a dramatic reduction in clutter.

## Megastore

**CLIENT:** Virgin Retail Ltd, London, UK

**DESCRIPTION OF PRODUCT:** Adaptable merchandise system and signing

**DESIGNER:** 20/20 Design and Strategy Consultants, London, UK

**PHOTOGRAPHER:** Jon O'Brien

**DATE OF COMPLETION:** May 1990

**TARGET MARKET:** 17–40

**PLACE OF SALE:** Virgin Megastores (Retailer)

**CLIENT'S BRIEF:** To create a shopping environment which would be as exciting and adrenalin-pumping as the music itself, including merchandise display systems with an in-built adaptability – allowing for both day-to-day and long-term shifts in demand for different audio and video formats.

**DESIGN RATIONALE:** This was driven by three issues: 1) to ensure that the customer could quickly arrive at the product of their choice; 2) to give a merchandizing system that was completely flexible to dynamic day-to-day requirements and to new format presentation; 3) to inject every part of the megastore with an all-pervading uniqueness.

## The "Tower"

**CLIENT:** Virgin Retail Ltd, London, UK

**DESCRIPTION OF PRODUCT:** 30-ft high steel audio visual tower

**DESIGNER:** 20/20 Design and Strategy Consultants, London, UK

**PHOTOGRAPHER:** Jon OBrien

**DATE OF COMPLETION:** May 1990

**TARGET MARKET:** 17–40

**PLACE OF SALE:** Virgin Megastore (retailer)

**CLIENT'S BRIEF:** To create a dynamic and dramatic signal to attract customers onto the first floor.

**DESIGN RATIONALE:** Three requirements for the main entrance to the store were identified: 1) to create a focal point for directional signage; 2) to form a structure that would consolidate all the audio/visual technology in a space that could be kept uncluttered; 3) to illustrate in an exciting way there was much more above.

## Chart Wall, Virgin Megastore

**CLIENT:** Virgin Retail Ltd, London, UK

**DESIGNER:** 20/20 Design & Strategy Consultants, London, UK

**PHOTOGRAPHER:** Jon O'Brien

**DATE OF COMPLETION:** July 1990

**TARGET MARKET:** Music and video customers, 25–40 years

**PLACE OF SALE:** Virgin Megastores

**CLIENT'S BRIEF:** Chart music still accounts for a large proportion of sales within the Megastores. Virgin wanted to develop a high-impact zone with a strong individual identity of its own, which would be dedicated to the display of these chart products – in all three formats (vinyl, CD and cassette).

**DESIGN RATIONALE:** The Chart Wall is located at the front of the store – a first port of call for the fast track shopper wishing to buy chart music. 20/20 used the same palette of materials used throughout the Megastore – but configured them in an individual way for the Chart Wall. This gives the area its individual identity, yet retains a link with the other departments in-store.

## The "Android"

**CLIENT:** Virgin Retail Ltd, London, UK

**DESCRIPTION OF PRODUCT:** Three-legged interactive computer games presenter

**DESIGNER:** 20/20 Design and Strategy Consultants, London, UK

**PHOTOGRAPHER:** Jon O'Brien

**DATE OF COMPLETION:** December 1990

**TARGET MARKET:** 12–25

**PLACE OF SALE:** Virgin Games Centres (retailer)

**CLIENT'S BRIEF:** To demonstrate computer games in such a way that the customer can play the game but the shop assistant can control how long he or she plays for. The unit had to be dramatic and attention-grabbing as well as practical.

**DESIGN RATIONALE:** The prime consideration was to move away from any "amusement arcade" connotations yet encourage the target market to interact with the Android. We employed the design vernacular of computer games in space-age styling, providing the customer with a slice of environmental realism which mirrors the visual fantasy experienced through the screen.

## The "Intelligent Wall"

**CLIENT:** Virgin Retail Ltd, London, UK

**DESCRIPTION OF PRODUCT:** Flexible, adaptable wall shelving system

**DESIGNER:** 20/20 Design and Strategy Consultants, London, UK

**PHOTOGRAPHER:** Jon O'Brien

**DATE OF COMPLETION:** December 1990

**TARGET MARKET:** 12–50

**PLACE OF SALE:** Virgin Games Centre (Retailer)

**CLIENT'S BRIEF:** To develop a wall shelving system that would be flexible enough to cope with a wide variety of different sized products and significant seasonal variation – particularly at Christmas.

**DESIGN RATIONALE:** The Intelligent Wall moves back and forth – and tilts. It expands and contracts to accommodate the required shelf depth, always keeping the merchandise in prime selling position and well presented. In addition, overhead graphic panels conceal storage compartments, enabling rapid replenishment of adjacent displays.

## Dances with Wolves

**CLIENT**: Virgin Megastore, Paris, France

**DESCRIPTION OF PRODUCT**: Point-of-sale display unit

**DESIGNER**: Bruno Synave, Paris, France

**DATE OF COMPLETION**: February 1992

**DESIGN RATIONALE**: To interpret the point-of-purchase material with the marketing concept so that it fitted the architecture of different sites.

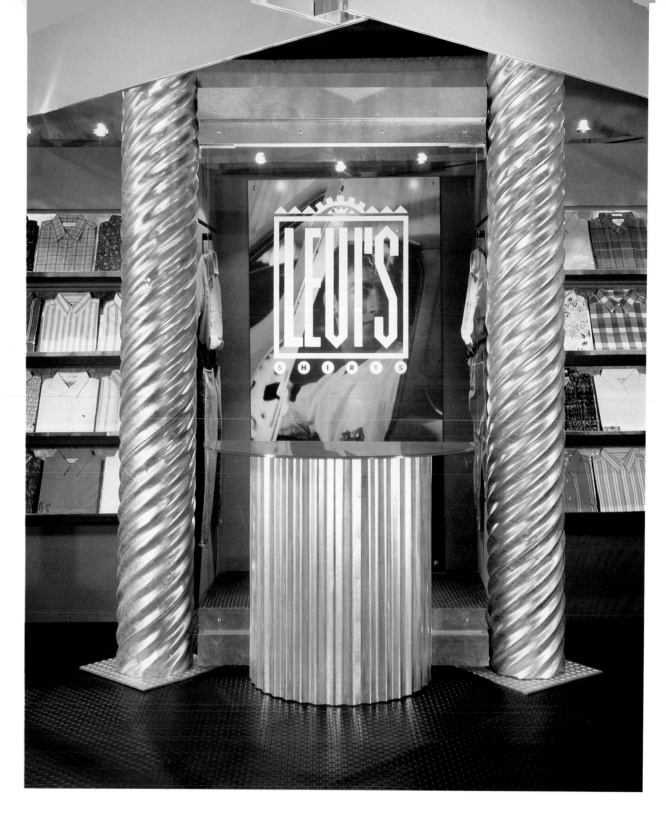

## Levi's Young Men's Shirts

**CLIENT:** Levi Strauss & Co, San Francisco, CA

**DESCRIPTION OF PRODUCT:** Materials: MR 16, lighting.
Pirelli flooring, Green plexi-glass, plywood

**DESIGNER:** Morla Design, Inc, San Francisco, CA

**ILLUSTRATOR OR PHOTOGRAPHER:** Jeanette Aramburu

**DATE OF COMPLETION:** January 1989

**PLACE OF SALE:** US department stores

**DESIGN RATIONALE:** This had minimal budget to
effectively merchandize a new line of Levi shirts for
young men. Construction techniques employed utilized

4ft × 8ft ½in edge-lit plexiglass with sand-blasted logo
applied to surface. Corrugated aluminum, galvanized
steel, and rubber tiling allowed for contemporary look
with minimum expense.

## Display Panels for In-store Presentation

**CLIENT:** Mothercare Ltd, London, UK

**DESIGNER:** RSCG Conran Design, London, UK

**DATE OF COMPLETION:** 1990

**TARGET MARKET:** Mothers of all ages

**PLACE OF SALE:** Mothercare retail outlets

**CLIENT'S BRIEF:** To create a sympathetic unified range of graphic material for all Mothercare outlets.

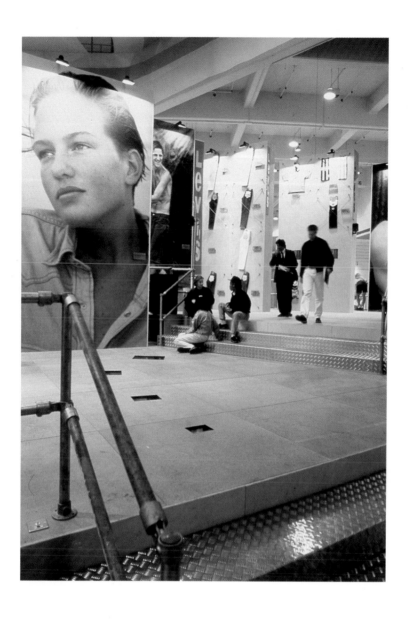

## Levi Jeans

**DESCRIPTION OF PRODUCT:** Exhibition for Levi jeans

**CLIENT:** Levi-Strauss, San Francisco, USA

**DESIGNER:** Checkland Kindleysides, Leicester, UK

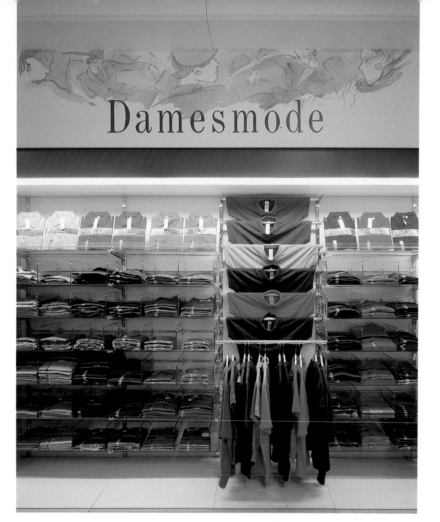

## Clothing & Household Linen

**CLIENT:** Hema, The Netherlands

**DESIGNER:** Davies & Baron, London, UK

**DATE OF COMPLETION:** November 1990

**TARGET MARKET:** Mass market retailing

**CLIENT'S BRIEF:** Hema is a Dutch variety store that has around 1500 different own-brand products. Davies & Baron's brief for the signage was to create atmosphere within product areas while retaining an overall homogeneous style. Therefore, illustrations were commissioned from Colin Barnes and combined with a bold typographic style.

Herenmode

Kindermode

## Top Man/Portfolio

**CLIENT:** Top Man, London, UK

**DESCRIPTION OF PRODUCT:** Menswear

**DESIGNER:** Davies & Baron, London, UK

**DATE OF COMPLETION:** 1989

**PLACE OF SALE:** Top Man outlets throughout the UK

**CLIENT'S BRIEF:** Top Man asked Davies & Baron to determine each one of the key clothing areas within its shops. The Davies & Baron graphics team, drawing influence from 1950s Americana, helped to segment the plethora of offers within Top Man.

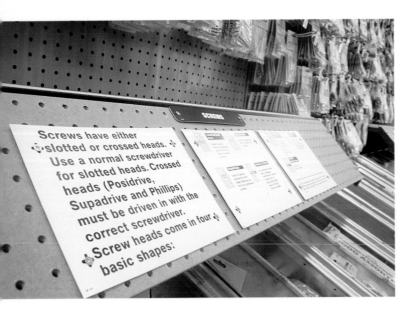

## Do-it-all Stores

**CLIENT:** W H Smith, London, UK

**DESIGNER:** RSCG Conran Design, London, UK

**DATE OF COMPLETION:** 1989

**TARGET MARKET:** Customers, predominantly male, interested in DIY

**PLACE OF SALE:** Do-it-all stores in the UK.

**PLUMBING IN A WASHING MACHINE**

**1** Position your machine close to a water supply pipe and a drainage outlet this will make DIY connection much easier.

**2** Supply connections can be made with self-cutting tap connectors; these can be fitted without turning the water off.

## Image Wall

**CLIENT:** Porsche Cars Great Britain Ltd, Reading, Berks, UK

**DESCRIPTION OF PRODUCT:** A series of 2-m high, modular panels manufactured from heat-formed foamex which can be configured in various combinations to form point-of-purchase displays.

**DESIGNER:** John Furneaux, Furneaux Stewart Design & Communication, London, UK

**PHOTOGRAPHER:** Nicholas Gentilli

**DATE OF COMPLETION:** 1989

**TARGET MARKET:** Official Porsche Centre customers

**PLACE OF SALE:** Official Porsche Centre Network (dealership network) in Great Britain and worldwide

**CLIENT'S BRIEF:** To design a complete point-of-purchase system, which would enhance product presentation, convey and make available knowledge of the Porsche product and therefore increase sales in the showroom.

**DESIGN RATIONALE:** The brief called for a semi-permanent yet inherently flexible design solution. The system needed to be sufficiently permanent to ensure that the client's products, services and corporate identity were correctly and consistently displayed, yet flexible enough to perform as space divider or pure point-of-purchase system whenever required.

# John Bell & Croyden

**CLIENT:** McCarthy plc, Leighton Buzzard, Bedfordshire, UK

**DESCRIPTION OF PRODUCT:** Comprehensive redesign and refurbishment of a flagship health-care department store servicing health-care professionals as well as retailing to the general public.

**DESIGNER:** XMPR International, London, UK

**DATE OF COMPLETION:** July 1989

**TARGET MARKET:** Health-care professionals, prescription and over-the-counter purchasers, and specialist and general pharmacy buyers.

**CLIENT'S BRIEF:** The objective was to help re-establish John Bell and Croyden as a leading market authority in the health-care sector. The project demanded a complete overhaul of all aspects of the interior and exterior of this prestigious site and the introduction of effective space management, customer circulation, merchandizing, display, lighting and signage systems.

**DESIGN RATIONALE:** The project commenced with a thorough planning and merchandizing analysis to ensure departments could be relocated and allotted space based upon potential revenue. A walkway was introduced to assist customer flows and merchandizing systems, and concessions were rationalized to evoke a stronger store personality.

## Sony Centre

**CLIENT:** Sony Europa GmbH, Cologne, Germany

**DESCRIPTION OF PRODUCT:** The Sony Centre is a specialist, authorized dealership retailing exclusively Sony products across Europe

**DESIGNER:** XMPR International, London, UK

**DATE OF COMPLETION:** April 1992

**TARGET MARKET:** Mainstream consumers seeking the same brand values inherent in the Sony brand – quality, attention to detail, and performance.

**PLACE OF SALE:** Sony Centres have already been introduced in Switzerland and the Netherlands, and are planned for other markets across Europe.

**CLIENT'S BRIEF:** To create a branded, aspirational retail offer exclusively merchandizing Sony consumer products. The scope of the project includes naming, visual identity, all aspects of merchandizing, point-of-sale, lighting and display, application to stand alone and shop-in-shop locations and the development of a European design manual.

**DESIGN RATIONALE:** The design scheme is, in essence, an extension of the Sony brand. The merchandizing system is extremely flexible and designed to direct attention primarily on to the product. Quality finishes, attention to detail and careful cable management avoid clutter and create a crisp environment.

## In-store Graphics

**CLIENT:** Mondadori Group, Milan, Italy

**DESIGNER:** Fran Lane, Landor Associates, London, UK

**ILLUSTRATOR OR PHOTOGRAPHER:** Jeff Fisher

**DATE OF COMPLETION:** Summer 1990

**TARGET MARKET:** Italian youth market: to encourage book purchase

**PLACE OF SALE:** Book shop owned by publishers

**CLIENT'S BRIEF:** To produce a new concept in book shop design and promotion that encouraged sale of books among Italian youth. To be positioned well away from the cold, serious and academic stance of existing book retailers.

**DESIGN RATIONALE:** The retail identity was kept deliberately classic and timeless to avoid change. It reflects the use of all the human senses in an environment that is warm, stimulating and fun. Retail point-of-sale graphics are highly visual and produced economically in order to be changed regularly.

Part of the promotion designed by Fran Lane for
Mondadori's own bookshop to encourage young Italians
to buy books.

Libri

Video

Quotidiani

Fotografia

Musica

Teatro

Regali

Novità

# Index of Products

**A**
Air miles  180
Alain Mikli Glasses  41
The Android  196
Giorgio Armani Glasses  29
The Art of Ballet  12
The Art of Christmas  13
The Art of Haute Couture  12
The Art of Music  12
The Art of Writing  14
Arthur et Lola  153
Athletics Equipment  42–3

**B**
Battistoni Cigarettes  65
Beer Mats  135
John Bell & Croyden  214–5
Best Direction Jeans  130
BHS Promotions  38–9
Boddington's Keg Bitter and Mild  134
Body Shop  22–25
Book Posters  17

**C**
Camcorder Demonstration Unit for JVC  66
Camcorder Bar  67
Camper Brutus  178
Carita  98–9
Caron Window Support  114
Chart Wall  194–5
Christmas Banners  19
City  166
Class Affair  127
Cleanse, Polish & Protect  25
Coca-Cola Coolers  156–7
Colour Correctives  24
Colour Tints  23
Complete Colour  24
Cool Clean Cucumber  23
Coral Betting Shop  52–55

**D**
Dances with Wolves  198–9
Decca Poster Series  26
Derma  154
Désirade  106
Dillons  181
Dillons Christmas Display  30
Dillons Easter Window Display  20
Display Panels for Mothercare  201
Display Cachou Lajaunie  164

**E**
Essilor Glass  121
Extinct is forever  24

**F**
Four Corners  44
Fuzzy Peach  22

**G**
A Gift of a Tree  161
Golden Beauty  90

**H**
Health & Beauty  186–7
Honda Freestanding Display  72

**I**
I Believe  140
Image Wall  80
Ingrid Millet  112, 113
In-store Graphics for Mondadori  218–9
The 'Intelligent Wall'  197

**J**
Jacques Dessage Make-up Stand  74

**K**
"K"  188
Killer Loop Sunglasses Display  122

**L**
LA Looks Cosmetic Kit  160
L'Art de Vivre  141
Lauren Product Glorifier  119
L'espace Valrhona  82
Letraset  170
Levi's Young Men's Shirts  200
Life is a Beach  23
Little Cobbler  132
London Life  144–5

**M**
Megastore  192
Michael Jackson Video  149
Miele Black Diamond  76
Mostly Men  25
My First Sony  62–3

**N**
Natwest Car Loans  182–3
Natwest Students  146
Natwest Gold Plus  147
No 7 Make Up  93

**O**
Obsession Tester Units  104–5
Oddbins Posters  58–9
Oh My Goodness  172
Ombre Subtile Eyeshadow  107

**P**
Paloma Picasso, Travelling Exhibition  78
Polaroid camera  124
Polaroid Promotion  40
Porto Quinta da Noval  126
Puirforcat  70

**Q**
Quad Hi-Fi Product Range  34–35

**R**
Rapport  92
React  88
Rogé Cavaillès Soap  151
Rose Cardin  94
Rowenta Irons  189
Royal Blue Window Display  138
Rucanor Shoe Display  129

**S**
Sample Suitcase, Golden Beauty  118
Sara Midda Promotion  148
Sarah Coventry Jewelry  151
Sarah Coventry Small Leather Goods  162
Sarah Coventry Sunglasses  77
Second Image Jeanswear  **184**
Seven-Up Giant Bottle  158
Shiseido Make up  64
Shiseido  100–101
Shiseido Window Support  115
Signage to Advertise Retail Space  46
W H Smith Do-it-all  208–211
Sola Clip-On  137
Sony Centre  216–7
Sony Mini Hi-Fi System  56–7
Sony Video Camcorder  68
Store Promotion Christmas for Paperchase  48
Studio Line Ravviva Ricci  155
Sunglasses Display  120
Systema Hair Care  174–5

**T**
Ténéré; Calandre  103
Theme Posters for Threshers  36–7
Tibere Watches  136
Times Watches  167
Tops  169
The Tower  83
Traction Production Glasses  123
Trifari Jewelry Fixture  150
Trifari Tune-In  133
Trucco Cosmetics  110–111

**U**
Ultrabrite  159

**V**
Visolaire  168

**W**
Weiss Art Products Unit  81
Who Do We Think We Are  22
Clothing for Hema  206–7

# Directory of Practising Designers

This directory lists the addresses of designers in current practice. While every effort has been made to ensure that this list was correct at the time of going to press, subsequent changes in address or status are beyond the publishers' remit.

**Alrec PoS Design**
PO Box 260, 3640 A6, Mijdrecht
The Netherlands
PRODUCT: Ruc anor Shoe Display 129

**Arnell-Bickford Associates**
New York, 10012, USA
PRODUCT: Killer Loop Sunglasses Display 122

**Ateliers Réunis**
214 rue Etienne Marcel, Bagnolet, France
PRODUCTS: Miele Black Diamond 76; Arthur et Lola 153

**Barry David Berger**
Associates Inc, 54 King Street, New York, NY10014 USA
PRODUCTS: Sarah Coventry Sunglasses 77; Sarah Coventry Small Leather Goods 162; Timex Watches 167; Letraset 170; Rowenta Irons 189

**Big Active Ltd**
D4 Metropolitan Wharf, Wapping, London E1 9SS
PRODUCTS: Second Image Jeanswear 184-5; Best Direction Jeans 130

**Body Shop**
Elsley Court, 20-22 Great Titchfield Street, London W1P 7AD
PRODUCT: Fuzzy Peach etc 22-24

**Buchanan Group**
11 Narborough Wood Park, Desford Road, Enderby, Leicester LE9 5XT
PRODUCTS: Camcorder Bar 67; JVC Camcorder Demonstration Unit 66; Honda Freestanding Display 72

**Clarke Hooper Consulting**
8 The Grove, Slough SL1 1QP, Berkshire
PRODUCT: Sony Mini Hi-Fi 56-7

**RSCG Conran Design**
The Clore Building, 4 Maguire Street, London SE1 2NQ
PRODUCTS: Quad Hi-Fi 34; Display Panels for Mothercare 201; WH Smith Do-it-all 208-211

**Consumer Promotions Inc.**
520 South Fulton Avenue, Mount Vernon, New York, 10550, USA
PRODUCTS: Obsession Tester Counter Units 104-5; Lauren Product Glorifier 119

**Corey McPherson Nash**
9 Calens Street, Watertown, MA 02172, USA
PRODUCT: Michael Jackson Video 149

**CR Communication & Design Services**
Reina Victoria, 24, Barcelona, 08021, Spain
PRODUCT: Camper Brutus 178-9

**Davies & Baron**
12 Goslett Yard, London WC2H 0EE
PRODUCTS: Hema 206-7; Top Man 208-9

**Design Field Pty Ltd**
1 Caledonia Street, Paddington, NSW 2021, Australia
PRODUCT: Weiss Art Products Unit 81

**Ekonos**
Paris, France
PRODUCT: Jacques Dessange Make-up Stand 74

**Paul Flum Ideas Inc**
11100, Linpage Place, St Louis, MO 63132, USA
PRODUCTS: Coca-Cola Coolers 156-7; Seven-Up Giant Bottle 158

**Furneaux Stewart Design & Communication**
24 Beaumont Mews, London W1N JLN
PRODUCT: Image Wall for Porsche 80

**Robert P. Gersin Associates**
11 East 22 Street, New York, NY, USA
PRODUCT: Oh My Goodness 172

**Jones & Co Design Ltd**
Greenland Studio, 9 Greenland Street
London NW1 0ND, UK
PRODUCT: Health & Beauty 186-7

**Stuart Karten Design**
4222D Glencoe Avenue, Marina del Rey, California 90292, USA
PRODUCTS: Trucco Cosmetics 110-111; Systema Hair Care 174-5

**Keeble & Hall**
Holy Innocents Church, Paddenswick Road
London W6 0UB
PRODUCT: Store Promotion – Christmas 48-50

**KMD Marketing**
140 Queens Road, Leicester LE2 3FS
PRODUCT: No 7 Make-up 93

**Light & Coley Ltd**
20 Fulham Broadway, London SW6 1AA
PRODUCT: Coral Betting Shops 52-5

**Landor Associates**
1001 Front Street, San Francisco, CA 94111
PRODUCT: In-store Graphics for Mondadori 218-221

**MBD Design**
11 rue Victor Hugo
Bagnolet, 93177 Cedex, France
PRODUCT: L'espace Valrhona 82

**Medallion Associates**
37 West 20th Street, New York, NY 10011, USA
PRODUCTS: Champs Sports Who's on first? 42-3; Reebok 84-5; I Believe 140

**Méthacryl**
11 bis, rue de St. Cloud, Suresnes, 95120, France
PRODUCTS: Shiseido Make-up 64; Ingrid Millet 112, 113; Caron Window Support 114; Shiseido Window Support 115

**Minale, Tattersfield Partners**
37 Sheen Road, Richmond TW9 1AJ, Surrey
PRODUCTS: Natwest Car Loans 182-3; Natwest Gold 147

**Morla Design Inc**
463, Bryant Street, San Francisco, California, 94107, USA
PRODUCTS: Wilkes Bashford Spring 89 Visual Identity 28; Levi's Young Men's Shirts 200

**Newell & Sorrell**
27 St Mary's Road, London NW10 4AS
PRODUCTS: Book Posters for Waterstones 16; Sherratt & Hughes Christmas Banners 18

**John Nowland**
122 Sturt Street, Adelaide, South Australia 5000
PRODUCT: Sola Clip-ons 137

**Nucleus Design**
John Loftus House, Summer Road, Thames Dutton, Surrey KT7 0RD
PRODUCT: Thresher Theme Posters 36-7

**Oakley Young 4th Dimension**
White acres, Whetstone Bus Park, Whetstone, Leicester LE8 3ZG
PRODUCTS: My First Sony 62; Sony Video Camcorder 69

**PLV Services Sailiard**
27 rue du Ballon, Noisy le Grand, 93160, France
PRODUCTS: Carita 98-9; Shiseido 100-101; Ténéré; Calandre 103

**Pat PLV**
79 Avenue du Président Wilson, Puteaux 92800, France
PRODUCTS: Alain Mikli Glasses; Rose Cardin 94; Désirade 106; Traction Production Glasses 123; Tibese Watches 136

**Proctor & Stevenson**
12 Cave Street, Bristol BS2 8RU
PRODUCT: Egypt Mortgage Promotion 19

**The Partners**
Albion Courtyard, Greenhill Rents, London EC1M 6BN
PRODUCTS: Decca Record Posters 26; Four Corners 45; Signage to Advertise Retail Space 46; Boddingtons Keg Bitter 134; Beer Mats 135; London Life 144-5

**Pethick & Money**
Studios 4 & 5, 75 Filmer Road, London SW6 7JF
PRODUCT: Rapport 92

**Prisme**
4 et 6 rue Curie, Suresnes, 92150, France
PRODUCTS: My First Sony 63; Puirforcat 70; Sony Dat Walkman 71; Paloma Picasso, Travelling Exhibition 78; Porto Quinta da Noval 126; Class Affair 127; Puirforcat 'Normandy' 131; Rogé Cavailles Soap 152

**Pentagram Design Ltd**
11 Needham Street, London W11 2RP
PRODUCTS: Polaroid Promotion 40; Polaroid Camera 124; Polaroid Sunglasses 125

**Maurice Progin**
Chandieu 22, CP68, CH 1000, Lausanne, Switzerland
PRODUCT: Battistoni Cigarettes 65

**Pyott Design Consultants Ltd**
4 Hanover Street, Waddon Village, Croydon CR0 1RR
PRODUCT: BHS Promotions 38

**Raison Pure**
38 rue Lantez, Paris 75011, France
PRODUCTS: Golden Beauty 90; Rouge Forever Lipstick 91; Sample Suitcase Golden Beauty 118

**RS Creation**
8 rue de Valmy, Montreuil 93100, France
PRODUCTS: Solars of Stendhal 75; Sunglasses Display 120; Essilor Glasses 121; Displays Cachou Lajaunie 164

**Smith & Milton**
Franklin House, 2 Millman Street, Kings Road, London SW10 0DA
PRODUCTS: Natwest Students 146-7; Air miles 180

**Studio DM Design**
Paris, France
PRODUCTS: Ombre Subtile Eyeshadow 107; Lancome products 108

**Studio John Boye**
Langergardvej 3, Rosen 7600, Struer, Denmark
PRODUCT: The Art of Ballet etc 12, 13, 14

**Studio Boncmi**
Via Lessolo, 19, Turin 10153, Italy
PRODUCTS: Derma 154; Ravviva Ricci 155

**Stocks Taylor Benson**
The Forge, Narborough Wood Park, Desford Road,
Endersby, Leicestershire LE9 5XT
PRODUCT: Dillons Window Display 20-21, 181

**Shimokochi/Reeves Design**
4465 Wilshire Boulevard, Suite 100, Los Angeles, CA,
90010, USA
PRODUCTS: LA Looks Cosmetic Kit 160; A Gift of a Tree
161

**Michael Sheridan & Co**
40 Nelson Street, Leicester LE1 7BA
PRODUCTS: React 88-9; Tops 169

**Stadium Design BV**
Post bus 408, 2180 AK, Hellegom, Netherlands
PRODUCT: Visolaire 168

**Stream-line**
10 Passage Ramey, Paris, 75018, France
PRODUCTS: Ultrabrite 159; City 166

**20/20 Design & Strategy Consultants**
78-80 Camden Street, London NW1 0EG
PRODUCTS: The Tower 82; Megastore 192; Chart Wall
194-5; Android 196; The 'Intelligent Wall' 197;
Dances with Wolves 198-9

**Trans World Marketing**
360 Murray Hill Park Way, East Rutherford, NJ 07073,
USA
PRODUCTS: Trifari Tune-In 133; Trifari Jewellery 150;
Sarah Coventry Jewellery 151

**XMPR International**
151 Freston Road, London W10 6TH
PRODUCTS: John Bell & Croydem 214-5; Sony Centre
216-7